Praise for The Dis

"It's very seldom that a new i
the potential to radically enhance team and org
performance. *The Discovery Prism* is that new idea! Anne and
Helen have delivered what I believe to be a 'best in class'
leadership tool for 21st century leaders. You must have it in your
leadership toolbox!"

Tom Pirrone
Senior Vice President, World View Enterprises, Inc., USA

"The challenge before every leader is to expand thinking and
align actions in service to stakeholders. *The Discovery Prism*
provides a practical framework that supports expanded thinking,
stakeholder alignment and collaboration as organizations
navigate the VUCA world."

Mary Ellen Rogahn
Senior Vice President, Global Coaching, Lee Hecht Harrison

"An extremely useful guide giving insights into how to enhance
your organisation, your teams and every individual contributing to
your overall success. A refreshing look at the power of individuals
and exploring ways to get the very best outcomes, collectively
and individually. This can only give positive results, with an
engaged workforce with keen interest in the strategic intent of an
organisation and feeling as if they play a part in the future success."

Steve Hails
Director of Health, Safety & Wellbeing, Thames Tideway Tunnel, UK

"*The Discovery Prism*© is a practical guide on how to implement
coaching analysis at the organizational level. It's a toolkit for
reaching results through a concrete methodology around
organizational culture. It's permeated by concepts of dialogue and
collaboration, as keys to good organizational insights. Definitely
a valuable read for leaders who want to have an impact, and for
people who believe in the power of personal values."

Francesca Romana Marcucci
Head of People & Culture Development, WWF International

"What I really like about *The Discovery Prism* is it provides the simple framework to help individuals, teams and organisations to ask those valuable questions; where they are now, what they are leaving behind and where they want to go in the future, which really helps to view the future with greater clarity and certainty. All too often these important questions are forgotten and the focus on the bigger purpose becomes secondary to the day to day task and output focused mind set. The framework really helps you evaluate what is important to your people and to remind us all about being accountable to yourself for the results you want to see."

Kirstie Loveridge
Senior Vice President, Human Resources, AEG Europe

"The understanding of leadership and organisational development is vast – and still at least one book has been missing so far. In *The Discovery Prism*, Anne Stenbom and Helen Battersby of GBL take us on a both philosophical and practical journey into the fundamentals of leadership and organisation. This is a holistic approach into seeing the roles of individuals, teams, and organisations and into how and where they can contribute. The intersection of different lenses define the legacy, promises and strategy of the organisation, yielding to a prism where the real fundamentals emerge. By engaging, in presence, you will be guided to understanding what is really important in each state or situation for the organisation. For me, experienced in futures thinking, scenarios, and vision building, this book gives me further understanding and tools for strengthening organisations for the future. It should be a required reading for any leader who wants to develop their organization holistically."

Ulf Boman
Future Strategist and Partner, Kairos Future, Sweden

"The authors present a simple framework that supports joined-up thinking. This is imperative for businesses to perform in our complex, ever-changing environment. It shows a way forward, through collaborative practices, to create workplaces where people can give their best service now and for the future. Essential reading for those who want to be part of building a powerful 21st century organisation!"

Michael Rask
Director Wafer Fab, Finisar Sweden AB

"Companies embrace change to survive in the market and it's hard for employees to bridge their understanding of strategic intent against the reality of their day-to-day. Senior management speak is not always easy to interpret and in the midst of the daily routine it is hard to connect what you do, to what the company says it wants to be and how it intends to get there. The aim of *The Discovery Prism©* in providing a framework for a clear, consistent and shared understanding of how strategy is delivered is unique, novel and long overdue. Any organisation that is serious about delivering its strategy must recognise that people are the key to delivering change, whilst keeping the lights on. *The Discovery Prism* provides a strong mechanism for involvement at all levels and the means of ensuring that terminology is understood up, down and across any organisation and then providing an environment where people can take responsibility and thrive without fear."

Geoff Pinch
Change Environment Leader, UK

ANNE STENBOM and HELEN BATTERSBY

THE
DISCOVERY
PRISM

A FRESH LENS ON 21ST CENTURY ORGANISATIONS

Printed in the United Kingdom
First Printing January 2019

First Edition

ISBN: 978-1-9164894-8-6 (Print)
ISBN: 978-1-9164894-9-3 (eBook)

Librotas Books
Portsmouth
Hampshire
PO2 9NT

We dedicate this book, in love and gratitude, to Edwin Derrick Lofthouse and Alan White, who as leaders and fathers have given us so much more than they ever had.

Acknowledgements

We would like to highlight authors who have inspired us greatly. We feel we are part of a wave of organisational and leadership thought leaders who see the organisation as profoundly human: where potential can be limited or maximised by many of the same factors that derail or maximise potential in individuals. Instead of a hero CEO these thought leaders recognise and champion the capacity of collaborative, aligned working to achieve extraordinary performance. Instead of reacting to the increasing complexity of the world by creating more processes, greater hierarchies, reinforcing command and control, winners and losers, this wave of experts talk about humility, emergence, transformational learning, presence, and maximising potential.

We would like to mention a few of these prominent influencers: Frederic Laloux: *Reinventing Organizations*; Alan Seale: *Create a World that Works*; Graham Leicester and Maureen O'Hara: *Dancing at the Edge: Competence, Culture and Organization in the 21st Century*; Joseph Jaworski: *Synchronicity: The Inner Path of Leadership*; Richard Barrett: *Liberating the Corporate Soul*; Jefferson Cann and Nigel Linacre: *An Introduction to 3 Dimensional Leadership*; Peter Hawkins: *Leadership Team Coaching* and Leandro Herrero: *Viral Change*. Along with many others all have, in their own unique ways, been supporting and inspiring change agents within the business realm and society.

Finally with deep love and gratitude, we would also like to acknowledge the contribution of our deceased and beloved co-founder of Global Business Leaders (GBL), Chris Monk.

Thanks

We would also like to thank those who kindly read chapters and whose feedback led to improvements in the book: Mike Battersby, Jenny Brett-Phare, Ken Charman, Geoff Pinch, Oscar Stenbom, Oliver Stenbom and Kerstin Wejlid. Too numerous to mention individually, thanks to all of those who allowed us to share stories, quotes and examples as well as those who provided testimonials. For professionalism, guidance and support we are grateful to our book mentor Karen Williams, editor Louise Lubke Cuss, designer Sam Pearce and to John Caswell for designing our cover. Finally thanks to our families whose patience and encouragement were invaluable: Svante, Oscar, Oliver and Eric; and Mike, Tom and Millie.

Contents

Foreword

The Space In Between

In *The Discovery Prism*, Helen Battersby and Anne Stenbom invite organizations into deeper and more expansive awareness and propose a new approach for discovery, understanding, strategy, and action. What I love about the Discovery Prism© is the inherent relationship spaces in the overlap lenses. As leaders and coaches, our most powerful and impactful work happens in the relationship spaces – in the spaces in between people, between people and situations, between people and ideas or beliefs, between one idea and another or one philosophy and another, between situations and groups, and the list goes on. These are the connecting points for everything.

It's not enough to know only what big topics should be addressed; breakthrough and transformation actually happen in the spaces in between the big topics. Part of the brilliance of the Discovery Prism© is that the overlap spaces of Strategy, Promises, and Legacy invite us into the "in between" spaces. These are the spaces where relationship actually happens. The names of each of these overlapping spaces give us direction and focus for the broad topics of conversation that are necessary if people and organizations are going to thrive in their purpose, vision, and service.

In the Prism in the center of the framework, everything comes together. What emerges in this central relationship space is determined first by the level of clarity in defining the three circular lenses, and then further refined by the quality of energy in the overlapping relationship spaces. Taking time for the step-by-step dialogue and exploration that the framework invites ultimately leads to the discovery of the full spectrum of the whole system. That central prism becomes a fountain of light pouring out over the entire system, nurturing and calling forth the best from all.

As I read, it occurs to me that in order for the most dynamic and generative explorations to happen, first in the circular lenses, and then in the overlapping spaces, the leaders, coaches, and facilitators must create spaces where those whom they serve and those with whom they collaborate feel full permission, freedom, and encouragement to explore, experiment, and learn.

All systems – families, communities, companies, countries, and even the world – are built on matrixes of relationships. Everything is connected to everything else. Everything. The idea behind the concept "six degrees of separation" is that nothing in the world – or in organizations and business – is separated from anything else by more than six connecting points in between. This is the underlying theme of the book – the interconnectedness of all people and all parts of the system. The Discovery Prism© is about consciously engaging with the relationships inherent in the system.

The Japanese concept of *Ma* can help us understand the significance of the relationship space – the space in between. *Ma* can be described as empty space – as a gap between one thing and another, or as a pause within movement or flow.

Yet it's much more than just empty space, a gap, or a pause. Ma does not actually describe a physical space created by objects, boundaries, or structures. Instead, *Ma* describes the *essence of the energy or intention that is felt or experienced in that space.* Intentionally creating and harnessing that energy for the benefit of the organization and its stakeholders is the whole premise of the Discovery Prism© work.

Ma is empty space that can be filled with any possibility. What you project into that space – an object, an intention, or an awareness or understanding – shapes the experience of anyone who enters into or engages with that space. You can intentionally infuse the space around or within a particular situation (the *Ma*) with a particular energy or consciousness.

For example, in a difficult situation, you might choose to hold a space of clarity, safety, care, or well being for others. In a project team, you might create an innovative environment where people are encouraged to experiment with new approaches and not worry about whether or not they will work. The key is to recognize the *Ma* that will best support what is needed or wanted in a particular situation, and then infuse the situation with that energy.

The point is that we can be conscious about the kind of *Ma* or energetic space we want to create. We can sense what is needed in the moment – what will serve the situation in the best way – and respond. Do we need stillness and quiet to allow us to drop into deeper awareness, understanding, feelings, and emotions? Or do we need high energy, excitement, and definitive action? Or something else?

An old Japanese poem (author unknown) beautifully illustrates what *Ma* is:

> *Thirty spokes meet in the hub, though the space between them is the essence of the wheel.*
>
> *Pots are formed from clay, though the space inside them is the essence of the pot.*
>
> *Walls with windows and doors form the house, though the space within them is the essence of the house.*
> (Reference: https://wawaza.com/pages/when-less-is-more-the-concept-of-japanese-ma.html)

In the same way, an organization is more than the balance sheet, the share price, the sales figures, the customers, or the staff. Its essence is felt between the people – between the departments, teams, and the full range of stakeholders. Thriving companies and organizations invite, encourage, and support relationships between stakeholders. Those relationships are the essence of organizational presence. This is the heart of the Discovery Prism.

The more you work with this concept of *Ma*, the more you can become intentional about the spaces in between in all aspects of your leadership and life. It provides a simple yet powerful way to create clear, intentional, and supportive spaces in between us and the people and situations in our lives and work.

As you dive into the riches that Helen and Anne share, keep this concept of Ma in your awareness. At the end of every chapter, pause to reflect on the ideas presented and the energetic spaces needed to put those ideas into practice within yourself and in support of those you serve.

Alan Seale, Director of the Center for Transformational Presence

Author of *Transformational Presence: How To Make a Difference in a Rapidly Changing World* and *Create a World That Works*

Introduction

Introduction

All real change is grounded in new ways of thinking and perceiving. While institutions matter, how they operate arises from how we operate, how people think and interact.
Peter Senge[1]

Our intention for this book is that it inspires people in organisations of any size to create something more powerful and exciting for the future. This starts with people being accountable to themselves for the results they want to see and for the context they work with and create daily. This book is for those who realise that the connection between the why and the how are key to get to a different what. It is for leaders in organisations who are keen to thrive in the 21ˢᵗ century.

We are Anne and Helen, both business leaders, executive coaches and facilitators working together within Global Business Leaders (GBL). We have numerous years of experience working inside and outside organisations. Our clients come from a broad spectrum of industries, of all colours, shapes and sizes and yet we encounter similar issues time and time again: "It's the people, silly!"

This book is about uncovering and realising emergent potential, individually and collectively, to create workplaces which are productive, fulfilling, and which make a difference to a wide range of stakeholders including future generations.

As coaches we ask a lot of questions in the firm belief that curiosity and exploration will allow the best of you to emerge. We take a positive strengths-based approach to all our work with individuals, their teams and organisations.

We work systemically. This means helping you to have a wide-angle view of the team or organisation as an entity and in its context so that you can create an environment of trust. This will allow you to focus on allowing what's important to surface and to then focus on what emerges. The role of the coach is to hold up the mirror to generate greater awareness about how the team or entity operates internally and is perceived externally.

We believe that awareness is the starting point for change and that what we focus on will influence what we get in return i.e. what we give is what we get. This requires time and space for reflection and thus a good deal of patience and trust. In the stretched and fast-paced business environments in which we work this seems counterintuitive and yet is the best, if not only way to tap into the creative potential organisations need to uncover for sustained, inspired performance.

The Discovery Prism© – a fresh lens on 21st century leadership

The Discovery Prism© framework we have created gives structure and focus to the discussions that need to happen for people to thrive in organisations. Each lens of the Prism represents a different theme that needs consideration in itself as well as how it connects to the other lenses. The Prism is chosen as a metaphor because it concentrates all the component colours into a powerful white light. The energy that is produced when all lenses have had focused attention and shine at their brightest represents a tangible force that is greater than the sum of the parts.

Figure 1 **The Discovery Prism**

The Discovery Prism© promotes an emergent discovery process that centres around the key questions: who are we here to serve and why?

The framework is question based; it provides no prescriptions. Answering the questions helps leaders and their teams define what is present and what needs to be preserved or changed to serve all stakeholders. It brings together the hard and the soft, the tangibles and the intangibles, the head, heart and soul[2] of individuals in their team and organisation. When people discuss the things that matter, a shared understanding and meaning is achieved. By using consistent language greater clarity is possible, reducing the misunderstandings that damage relationships and undermine performance. In this way, the discovery work (the collaborative undertaking of exploring the lenses) supports the connections across that organisation and to its stakeholders, since the answers cannot be arrived at alone.

The framework acknowledges the dynamic influence of time. It helps individuals and teams to enquire into where they are now, what they are leaving behind and where they want to go in the future. *The past* is where you acknowledge what has served well, what should be preserved and what is no longer needed (especially in legacy, core values and strategy). *The present* is where the lenses will reflect the individual and collective experience of work in the current context. *The future*, especially purpose, promises and core values, will draw on aspects of aspiration, development and realisable potential.

What the Prism at the centre illuminates will be different for each organisation. We believe it will give new insights to enable the organisation to view the future with greater clarity and certainty. As organisations engage with the Discovery Prism© they become more self-aware, purposeful and connected – a conscious whole.

Who is this book for?

This book is inspired by a response to the challenges faced by our clients.

It is for heads of organisations who recognise they can't predict what is going to happen in their line of business and realise no one person can do the job – they want to tap into everybody's expertise and resources to take everyone forward.

It is for those who have taken the team to a point where performance has improved but they know there is still more to be achieved. They know there's more that they can access to navigate the complexity within and without the organisation.

It is for those who want to harness the sustained interest of the younger generation who are inspired by collaboration, co-creation, purpose and values that are lived.

It is for those who have experienced off-the-shelf leadership training (time management, influencing, delegation...) but do not know what is different and unique about themselves and how they impact their environment.

It is for those who, even as they are taken up with the day to day without a minute to lift their heads, know the doing is not enough.

What our clients want is to deal with challenges with ease and grace. To know they can cope with any situation and that the unknown is normal. They want less stress and to make sense of complexity. They want to dare to deal with the stuff that matters to people, with a common language to talk about what is important but hard to talk about. They want to increase their bandwidth to look at wider patterns whilst remaining grounded in the present. They want hope for a better future, not just for themselves but for a far wider community.

What's new about the Discovery Prism©?

Wisdom is not about knowing more but about knowing with more of you.
The Rev. Dr. Cynthia Bourgeault

Frameworks are a way of breaking complex things down into manageable components, allowing focus on parts of the system while keeping the whole in view. There are already many business frameworks in existence and you may reasonably wonder why we have brought one more into the mix.

In answering the "What is new" question, we are aware of the tremendous body of work in existence of which we have covered only a fraction, no matter how prolific our reading. Experienced leaders in organisations, education and business coaches who have commented on our work, have singled out the following aspects as most significant in the Discovery Prism©:

- It brings together tangibles and intangibles in a practical way
- It ensures businesses do not potentially limit the lenses they do have in place by missing connections to other lenses
- It connects what is important to the individual as well as the collective
- It incorporates what's important from the "influential past" and the "grounded present" in order to grasp future potential
- It focuses quickly on important gaps in strategic thinking

To give an example, one HR professional in a large multinational in the financial services industry had been working with her team for a significant period to prepare for the sale of the company. Looking at the Discovery Prism© she immediately noted that they had been so focused on the sale being the main objective that they had not worked on the bigger purpose that would sustain their people through to the other side of the transaction. She knew it was important to address. The rapidity with which she identified a neglected area meant the issue was near the surface, manifesting itself in challenging employee behaviours. The Discovery Prism© helped her pinpoint the root of a problem requiring attention.

Being versus Doing

In leadership development programmes one of the first exercises we set our participants is to come up with characteristics, attributes and traits of the average leader versus a superior one. Despite this being an early exercise we are struck by how participants classify the differences. For the average leader the typical list includes:

- Output/target driven
- Hard worker
- Goal-oriented
- Guided by own interests

- Lack of personal interest in others
- Top-down style

In short, the average leader is results-oriented and hard-working but not that interested in people or in developing the team. The superior leader is typically described as:

- Trusts and develops trust
- Inspires, motivates
- Authentic, walks the talk
- Has a vision
- Is a great team builder

These lists differ in two important respects. For the average leader (note we do not ask for the characteristics of a bad leader) the emphasis is on task and the perceived focus is self, whereas the superior leader is described in terms of what he or she *is* – their "being" – and they are perceived as being other-focused which in turn releases the wider potential of others (the dividend of being trusted, trusting, inspired and motivated).

Instinctively, the "being" (walking the talk, authenticity, being inspirational, visionary, trustworthy and caring), is held to be important despite that, in many organisations, task and output are considered more regularly worthy of note and reward e.g. meeting sales targets, completing a project. It seems, when given the opportunity to reflect, people instinctively know aspects of the "being" are important e.g. how leaders engage with their team and how they develop, how enthusiastic, energetic and resourceful teams are as a result. We feel that the being aspects of an organisation are also critical in creating a superior (full potential) organisation which has capacity to thrive in the 21st century.

We also know that the "being" – the essence of the organisation – is about more than one individual or one team. When individuals describe the best place they've worked at, they'll often cite a sense of unity, of working as a team, pulling in the same direction, feeling a part of something they're proud of. They also mention having the space and confidence to be creative and feeling a positive energy that is contagious. Obtaining this alignment across the organisation and across the borders of the organisation to wider stakeholders is in our view part of harnessing productive and collective energy to create a dynamic, present organisation.

Organisational presence

What do we mean by a present organisation? A way of understanding this concept is to think of personal presence. When a person is said to be present they are referring to more than a physical body occupying space (we may remember replying "present" in answer to the teacher calling our name each morning at school when it meant anything but). Being present is being totally attuned. There is an awareness of what's going on outside of you, and simultaneously what is going on inside of you, while being able to regulate the inner to enhance the impact on the outer. When you are present there is an absence of stories in your head either calling up the past or running away to the future. Call it a way of being totally "tuned in" to the moment.

This kind of presence has transformational potential. You can listen deeply and sense the underlying meaning. You can see without prejudice. By removing your "clutter" (preconceptions and running commentary) you expand your own space and can open up to what might emerge. You can tap into your intuition, allowing deep connection to yourself and to others. This kind of presence allows the creation of the possible and potential rather than the predictable or the probable.

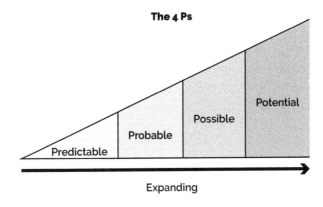

Figure 2 **The 4 Ps** (Source unknown)

The 4 Ps diagram shows how the wedges expand in size from the predictable to the potential. If we do what we've always done (to paraphrase the famous Einstein quote) we'll get what we've always got. We'll stay in our "predictable" or "probable" small space. The transformational space created by organisational presence allows us to expand possibilities, maximise resources, and thrive rather than survive. This happens by many people being "present" and having the kind of conversations that matter. The paradoxical nature of presence is that by being grounded in the present, you are given the clarity to see creative paths to the future. As coaches we see examples of this inherent creativity each time we work with a client. Asking questions leads to discovery, to new thoughts and ideas. Our potential is most often stunted by self-limiting beliefs about our own human brilliance. Any kind of development, whether personal or collective, involves the capacity to see the present clearly – to see the culture we're in. The first step to envisioning the future is to heighten awareness of the present.

Our concept of organisational presence is an organisation that is clear-sighted and alive to "what is" i.e. what is lived and experienced. Checking for alignment between the lenses of the Discovery Prism© acts as an organisational health check and a way of capturing and redeploying leaking energy. The organisation is then able to see the future more clearly because it is fully connected.

Sustainability and the Discovery Prism©

Sustainability is a key concept for all conscious and responsible organisations in the 21st century. It is one of GBL's core values and relevant from two perspectives. The first is that of human sustainability. This is about the inherent dignity and respect of every human being. This is not (and should not be) surrendered in any way when we join an organisation, or change because we are either customer or supplier. That dignity and respect should be honoured regardless of hierarchy or business relationship. In the words of a small business owner we interviewed:

> *I always try to be the same person regardless of who I'm speaking to (whether family, friends, colleagues, clients or site workers). Some people seem to think they have separate lives, they are not the same at work or home or out with friends. People are people, when we drill down, we all have the same issues.*
> Peter Gower, GD Partnership

The reflection of this value we call human sustainability is implicit in the Discovery Prism©. Inviting participation in each of the lenses is inviting human interaction at the deepest levels.

The second is systemic sustainability. This is about no organisation being an island. How far you stretch beyond organisational territory to consider stakeholders will depend on the business you are in. The micro to the macro could look like: individual, team, collaborating team, executive team, national team, international organisation, collaborating independent entities, community, nation, continent, planet. (In some organisations there are multiple levels of this e.g. manufacturing and sales outlets of the same organisation. Often, they consider each other as competing entities rather than partners serving the same stakeholders.)

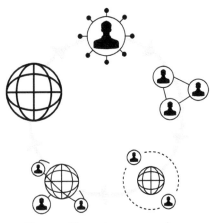

Figure 3 **The micro-macro loop**

There is a sense in which the impact on the individual is also an impact on the planet. Imagine a world populated by organisations who treated their workforce as commodities – how would those individuals then impact their communities? Imagine the reverse, a world populated by organisations where individuals flourished – what would be the chain reaction for communities and the planet? There is an inherent balance to sustainability whether it's in your sights or not. The micro always has an impact on the macro. Systemic sustainability is reflected especially in the lenses of stakeholders and legacy, and, of course, depending on your reach, may also appear in any of the other lenses.

Conclusion

(If) the burden of leadership in the modern age seems overwhelming, the potential benefits are overwhelming too. Large organizations – if led well – can do more for more people than they have at any other moment in history. That is the flip side of all the chaos, complexity, and pressure, and it makes leading through those challenges a noble endeavor.[3]
McKinsey Report

In today's VUCA (volatile, uncertain, complex and ambiguous) world nothing stands still for long. What makes it VUCA is well documented[4] and probably experienced by us all at some level:

- Adapting to rapid technological advances
- Geographical shifts in the engines of growth
- The inter-connectivity offered by the vast array of communication networks.

We believe there is a case to flag the 21st century business environment as markedly different to what has come previously. Our hyper-connected globe has blurred the lines between the economic, political and social such that organisations are no longer just economic entities. New generations entering the workplace increasingly look to their employment for more than just a way to earn a living.

Today, more than ever, leaders need the capacity to respond and adapt to emerging circumstances. They can no longer afford to lead and operate in the same predictable ways that may have brought them success in the past. Leaders, teams and organisations must learn to operate in this VUCA context both on the outside (the external market environment) and on the inside (the individual/team/organisational culture).

This interconnected environment also causes us to look at how success is evaluated. If it is based on the exploitation of people or of a wider community then it is not inherently sustainable in either human or environmental terms.

The key to survive and thrive in the future depends on how we engage with the flux and find new creative responses by tapping into the abundance of positive energy we all possess.

Structure of the book

Each lens of the Discovery Prism© is a separate chapter. We start with the three circular lenses: purpose and values, vision, stakeholders and mission. From the overlaps of these three, a further three lenses are formed: promises, strategy and legacy. The final chapter describes the centre of the framework: the Prism.

In each chapter we explain what we mean by each term and illustrate this with examples of organisations as well as the kind of activity that can be run to discover more about the topic. We show how each lens provides meaning for other lenses and thus contributes to the whole. The case study examples are chosen to represent best practice (and a few cases of worst), in keeping with our definition of 21st century organisations. We refer to smaller and larger organisations, some we have worked with, others we have come across in our research.

At the end of each chapter some guiding questions have been formulated to give direction to the discussion and help in the choice of which intervention to pursue. The list of suggestions is not exhaustive and is intended as a starting point to discovery. Our hope is that you will have many inspired insights (and we would love to hear about them).

By working on each lens as a separate entity and in combination with other lenses you discover the Prism.

We have included a glossary of key terms we use frequently at the back of the book. We have highlighted in grey some of those terms as they appear.

CHAPTER 1

The Discovery Prism©

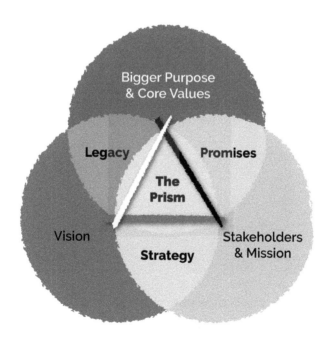

1. The Discovery Prism©

You create the path by walking it.
Chris Monk

The starting point for exploration using the Discovery Prism© framework is to focus on one of the three circular lenses. The questions in each respective chapter prompt an enquiry into current status and desired future outcomes. No existing organisation starts with a blank page and much work will already have been conducted in one or more areas. The review of what already exists can form the starting point for discussion and ensuing action. The outcome of the discovery work for each theme informs next steps and provides a platform on which the development journey builds.

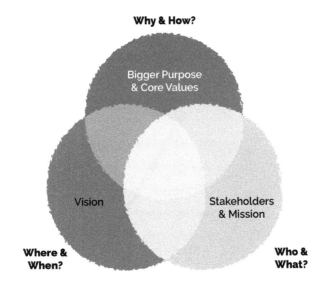

Figure 4 **The three circular lenses**

Three circular lenses

The first three of the circular lenses answer the questions sometimes known as the "fundamental questions", memorialised by Kipling in his *Just So Stories* (1902).

- Why and How? (bigger purpose and core values)
- Who and What? (stakeholders and mission[5])
- Where and When? (vision)

Being clear about the three circular lenses provides a solid foundation to understand the system in which an entity operates. Clarity about bigger purpose, core values, vision, mission and stakeholders can be used to guide decision-making.

Equally important in this process is to uncover what and who is not included in our answers to these big questions i.e. what is off limits and how we tackle something that is considered unacceptable. To be authentic we need to know what we are not, as much as what we are.

The overlap lenses

The three overlap lenses (highlighted in Figure 5 overleaf) are created where two of the circular lenses overlap. They are the sense checks on the coherence of the circular lenses from which they are formed. They are the glue that pulls the whole framework together to replace outdated one-dimensional thinking: command and control management, short-termism and organisational relationships that only benefit the few rather than serve the common good.

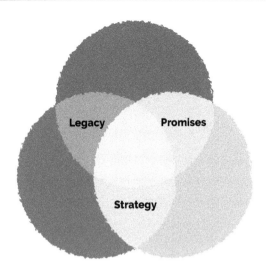

Figure 5 **The overlap lenses**

The three overlap lenses are:

Strategy: how to deliver the mission to stakeholders in keeping with the vision.

Promises: the synergy of the promises we make to ourselves internally (keeping true to our bigger purpose and values) and those we make externally to stakeholders.

Legacy: the intersection between vision and purpose – what we leave behind intentionally and positively for future generations.

The greatest concentration of current organisational focus is given to the three circular lenses. Vision and mission are the most commonly developed of them. Of the three overlap lenses, strategy is undoubtedly the frontrunner and its effectiveness can only be enhanced by ensuring alignment with stakeholders and longer term vision. People may think that promises is another word for brand and it is partially, but in a highly connected world transparency is a given and the failure to integrate promises made outside and inside the organisation is a perilous one. Legacy is rarely referred to and will become more important as we consider stewardship for future generations as an important part of the 21st century mindset.

The Prism at the centre where everything overlaps brings an added dimension to the framework.

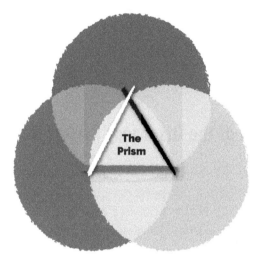

Figure 6 **The Prism**

The Prism

The Prism is formed at the centre of the framework. Quite simply, it's the emergent, whole-system space where everything comes together. The word "emergent" describes the whole as greater than the sum of its parts.

The Prism takes all the colours from the contributing lenses but loses nothing of their individuality, yet in coming together the colours are reflected as something different – a concentrated white light.

The Prism is a metaphor for the sum potential of all individuals in an organisation. It may be experienced as a powerful collective energy that is present when all elements are aligned. In the Prism chapter, we describe in more detail what can emerge from conducting the discovery work under the headings:

- Elevating the status of being
- Collaboration
- Dialogue
- Connecting the dots

Facilitation of the Discovery Prism© journey

The Discovery Prism© is practical in its application – it can apply to an individual (for personal congruence), a team or an entire organisation. In this book we concentrate on teams and organisations. The journey, facilitated via dialogue, is one where the individual's contribution is valued, encouraging participation and co-creation of the whole. This co-creation helps build trust, which is the foundation for deeper engagement and collaboration. The resulting organisational presence brings a collective wisdom which translates to outstanding performance. There is an emphasis on the doing **and** the being for effective and purposeful output, engagement and energy transfer from the individual to the team to the organisation and back to the team and the individual. A mutual energetic exchange.

Where you start on the **Discovery Prism©** will depend on specific needs of your organisation and where you wish the exploration to take you. There is no prescriptive process apart from starting with the circular lenses before going on to the overlaps. There is a logical sequence (1–4), see below, which could be repeated for each of the lenses, or could be completed in stages: no. 1 for all the lenses, no. 2 for all the lenses etc. It may be that you are drawn from one stage to the logical next, or even that you work on more than one lens at the same time. Note that no. 4 automatically leads back to no. 1 but at another level – an ever-expanding spiral.

Discovery Prism© stages

1. **Pre-exploration:** What is the intention for the upcoming work?
2. **Exploring the Discovery Prism©:** Creative reflection on the questions through dialogue and collaboration.
3. **Connecting the dots:** Distilling responses at the Prism to find the common essence. What paths are clear; what is now possible?
4. **Sustaining focus:** What needs to happen to keep the conversations and connections fluid and relevant and prevent complacency?

A question-based, facilitated framework

We recommend that the Discovery Prism© is externally facilitated by an impartial and trusted facilitator (initially at least as this will encourage openness amongst participants). It is question based to encourage reflection and participation. There are no right or wrong answers but there are responses which are grounded in real experience and others that are assumptions, born from denial or simple mistrust. It is the facilitator's job to create a safe space for sharing and to ensure that contributions are well founded. As participants become conscious of their present, acknowledging and releasing what holds them back, they become more able to consciously create the future through their experiences, insights and commitments.

Dialogue is needed to deeply explore and to engage participants. The implication of sharing not just from the head but from the heart and gut means that intuitive facilitation is as important as the logical understanding of the content. The facilitator's "presence" is a key factor within the whole system (knowingly or unwittingly).

The facilitator should model the behaviours he or she encourages in participants, holding the space and working with what emerges.

The inspiration for the Discovery Prism© comes from our distilled experiences, insights and reflection. In a sense, we have discovered the framework from our own exploration of the lenses at an unconscious level. We find those who have inspired us have organised and articulated something we already know deep down to be true. We hope you will find the same.

Working with the Discovery Prism© framework can help teams and organisations (a) as a diagnostic tool in exploring blocks to engagement and performance and (b) as a creative problem solver to overcome those blocks. The ways in which it can have an impact can be further defined as:

Increasing retention, engagement, and performance by

- Diagnosing and removing internal incongruences that limit performance
- Providing the catalyst for important conversations which engage your people
- Building trust through common exploration of core themes
- Building collaboration through alignment of purpose
- Creating alignment across the organisation to build attunement[6]
- Exponentially increasing the effectiveness of the organisation

Strengthening connection between the organisation and stakeholders by

- Creating alignment between the organisation and its stakeholders
- Creating alignment between internal culture and external brand
- Aligning core messages to stakeholders
- Attracting stakeholders who share purpose and values

Clarifying strategic direction of the organisation by

- Gaining clarity of the bigger picture affecting future steps
- Diagnosing the kind of leaders you want to promote, develop and engender in the organisation
- Considering stakeholder relationships more deeply
- Using all the lenses as a framework for decision-making

CHAPTER SUMMARY

Here are the main points of Chapter 1:

> An introduction to the Discovery Prism© framework, describing the circular lenses, the overlap lenses and the emergent nature of the Prism at the centre of the framework

> An explanation of the elements central to working with the Prism, amongst them wide participation, collaboration and dialogue

> An overview of how to work with the Discovery Prism© framework considering the four stages

> The importance of initial external facilitation for trusted impartiality

> The benefits that may accrue from working with the Discovery Prism©

CHAPTER 2

Bigger Purpose and Core Values

Why & How?

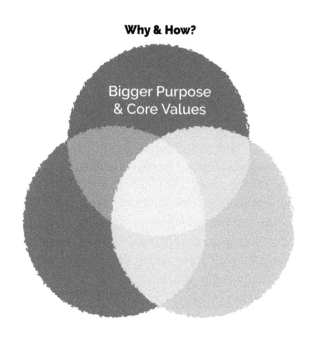

2. Bigger Purpose and Core Values

The least of things with a meaning is worth more in life than the greatest of things without it.
Carl Jung

Like the air we breathe, we can sometimes take the purpose of something for granted. We saw the direction of a board strategy change when a new financial director asked of an initiative, "Why are we doing this?" Another client, when pressed as to what was leading to his lack of trust of a new board member, surmised it was because he didn't yet know what his purpose was.

Purpose in the Discovery Prism© answers the question "Why?" It searches to know what is of value – what is important enough for you to want to be a part of something, to take action, to trust others and invest your time in working with them. Bigger purpose is the overarching and most exhaustive response you get from discovering why that is important (henceforth we will shorten it to purpose). Purpose and values are strongly interlinked. The definition of "values" could be summarised as what is important to us. We trust people who share our values. Our values are revealed in what we believe and in what triggers our emotional responses be they positive or negative.

Values are revealed ultimately in our behaviours. Take the two values of fairness and resourcefulness. A child takes the last biscuit, having enjoyed more than his playmates. One adult driven by a value of fairness may admonish the child for not sharing; another may congratulate him for being resourceful. Our sense of purpose will flow from our values. Together, bigger purpose and values form the upper part of our Discovery Prism© answering the questions Why? (Why am I here/Why are we here/Why do we exist together/What purpose do we serve) and How[7] are we being together (How do we act towards each other/What are our behavioural norms)?

Exploring purpose and values, then implementing the discoveries to guide the direction and behaviours of the organisation, is part of creating an aligned culture which supports the authenticity of the organisational brand externally (more of which in Chapter 5) and provides motivation and inspiration within. When communicated and integrated into the core of the business they will become signposts to attract talent, clients and potential collaborators.

We have noticed that what we call bigger purpose is often expressed by others as mission but in the Discovery Prism© is a separate lens. What is most important is not what it is called but how it is defined and the reflection that is prompted. At some level, all the lenses of the Discovery Prism© are heavily co-dependent. We agree that bigger purpose or mission[8], or whatever name is chosen, can elegantly express why we are here or what we are driven to. Here's an example from The Center for Transformational Presence:[9]

> *Why? – Our mission is simple: We create a world that works.*

And from Zappos:[10]

> *Our company's purpose statement is to live and deliver wow. We believe the highest level of achievement is to get somebody to say "wow". It's not whether we sold something on the website.*

For clarity we have separated this chapter into two sections, leading with bigger purpose and concluding with values.

Bigger Purpose: The Why

We will look at purpose from the following angles:

- The meaning of purpose and why it is important to individuals and the collective
- Why purpose-led organisations matter now more than ever
- The correlation between purpose and financial performance

Purpose – why it is important to individuals and the collective

Human beings are a meaning-seeking species, driven by the quest to find out "Why?" And it starts early in our development as any person who has been around a small child will know. That small child also knows that one "Why?" isn't enough. There are more layers to be uncovered to get to the underlying big WHY of something that is important. When thinking of an individual's or organisational purpose similar probing is often necessary to get to the big purpose. We call things that are buried under many layers "deep" – and it's this deep-down (bigger) purpose that we're aiming to uncover. As Laurens van der Post puts it:

> The Bushman storytellers talk about two kinds of hunger. They say there is physical hunger, then what they call the "Great Hunger". That is the hunger for meaning. There is only one thing that is truly insufferable, and that is a life without meaning. There is nothing wrong with the search for happiness. But there is something great – meaning – which transfigures all. When you have meaning you are content, you belong.[11]

If people are not living in accord with their deep-down, bigger purpose they may experience disconnection. Think of high earners who leave financial rewards to work as teachers to fulfil their purpose as educators and inspirers of young people. Think of people who leave the office to spend more time with their families (this is sometimes a euphemism for those expelled from office but it must be true some of the time). The bigger the correlation to the answer "Why are you here?" and the extent to which you fulfil that at work, the more likely you are to excel. The more likely an individual is to excel, the more likely an organisation is to thrive.

Purpose may or may not be where people start to connect the dots on the Discovery Prism©, but it is always an intrinsic part of aligning the whole (whether it concerns an individual or an organisation). This lens is one that looks inward (for the individual) and outward (for the organisation). It is crucial to align what an individual and the organisation see as important to realise the potential of both.

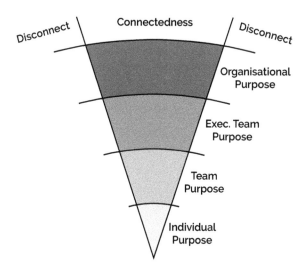

Figure 7 **Purpose spectrum for connectedness**

An essential element of 21st century organisations, large and small, is a consideration for sustainability in its widest sense. This of course incorporates the modern concept of environmental sustainability (modern perhaps for the Western world but for centuries at the heart of many older cultures such as the aboriginal and native American Indian cultures) as well as the age-old one of human sustainability. The latter has always been at the forefront in the best companies. It simply recognises our collective human dignity. This affects the remit of our bigger purpose, the integrity of our behaviour, the reach of our vision, the definition of our stakeholders and the ambition of our legacy.

In his book, *Start With Why: How Great Leaders Inspire Everyone to Take Action*,[12] Simon Sinek unpicks what makes someone or an organisation inspirational. He concludes that purpose is the central motivator, the answer to the question "Why" of the title. The "Why" is about what gets you up in the morning, a belief, a purpose. In the Discovery Prism© the big why is the bigger purpose.

Feeling connected to the purpose of the organisation is important for performance, and retention of personnel. It is important for optimum collaboration, especially in 21st century organisations. True collaboration is a result of trust and trust is built in knowing what is important to the people around you and the organisation you serve. Inspiration, engagement, retention, trust, collaboration – understanding purpose is a cornerstone on which all these factors are built.

A STORY OF PURPOSE

Donal Collins, a GP and 2015 Development Champion of the Year as voted by the Thames Valley NHS Leadership Development Academy, relates how changing the focus of the bigger purpose makes a huge difference. "If you have that (bigger purpose) everything makes sense." He is a partner in a group of three practices which act independently with an overarching business unity to make any client transfers between the different surgeries seamless.

The partners asked themselves the question, What are we really about? It was not, they decided, to maximise income but to improve the health of the population. How did this lead to different behaviours and what difference did it make to their stakeholders?

Donal gives Type 2 diabetes as an example. Research shows that the interventions taking place in the first five years of detection of the disease will make a huge impact on its manageability and outcomes for the patient (and expense for the state) in the long term. Doctors can provide advice on diet, exercise and raising activity levels and prescribe effective drugs but to reap the benefits, the patient also needs to participate in his or her recuperation. Doctors will still get paid if they show that they are making reasonable efforts to bring the patient into the surgery and so after three or four unanswered letters, the no-show patient is still a source of income. He tells of an inspirational surgery in the north of England, where, mindful of their own shift of purpose from maximising income to improving the health of the population, the doctors went a step further than letter writing. They asked themselves what they could and should do. They sent a text to all of their patients saying they were struggling to help them – help us to help you, the doctors pleaded.

The so-called super-attenders (patients who come into the surgery 24/25 times a year compared to the normal attenders 2/3) were the first ones to volunteer in response to the text. Groups of around 30 people formed to meet and walk, and share favourite recipes. These groups effectively created their own well-being centres. The reasons behind the super-attenders' prolific visits to the surgery were manifold – low mood, loss of self-esteem, no job – so the surgery was somewhere they could go. The surgery found that six months down the line from forming these groups the so-called super-attenders become frustrated with their own pairings and wanted to be surrounded with more positive people. They stopped coming to the surgery and this freed up time for the GPs meaning that they didn't have to recruit new people to deal with their existing patient base. In addition to saving recruitment costs, their weekly capacity to see patients was increased by 3.5%.

All because they focused on the purpose and not the bottom line (but the bottom line ended up improving as a result).

Helen asked Donal what the catalyst was for the change in focus. "Impending disaster," he answered. "Before you know there is nothing you can do, you keep doing the wrong things a bit righter – staying to work later, doubling your efforts, until there is nothing more you can do and everyone is exhausted anyway. Taking a deep dive into the data and becoming grounded in what is actually happening rather than what you all think is happening is the first step. What was most important in the process of change? Transparency of the process, putting on the table what concerned people about the changes and dealing with them, and having a coach to facilitate, who had no ego rather than for everyone to get a great result. We could trust that non-partisan facilitation."

Having a purpose that everyone understands, says Donal, makes things easier as it provides a template against which you measure everything. If you have an initiative or a proposal, you see if it aligns with the purpose. For Donal the bigger purpose lens is what matters most and from which all the others flow. The gain at the middle of the framework, the Prism, is everything "making sense".

Why purpose-led organisations matter now more than ever

The importance of purpose, whether it be purpose-led organisations or inspiring purpose-filled executives, has been advocated by top financial schools and institutions. They speak of the responsibility of wealthy corporations to multiple stakeholders through organisations whose purpose is defined not only by the scope of business activity but by the quality of the human relationships generated by them. They also suggest that those that are not purpose-driven will lose the interest of key stakeholders.

Addressing the London Business School at the 11th Private Equity Symposium[13], Professor Ioannis Ioannou advocated that the potential for businesses to have a positive impact has never been higher. He referred to figures from Global Justice Now[14] which show that of the largest 100 global economic entities, 69 of them are companies, not governments. The combined revenues of the top 10 of these companies are larger than the combined revenues of the 180 poorest countries together. The potential of corporations to amass such vast wealth and consequently wield great power uniquely positions them, if they so choose, to promote sustainable and inclusive growth. Companies such as Unilever (Purpose: To make sustainable living commonplace) believe that. They believe this is the best long-term way for their business to grow. Being purpose-led is not limited to large companies. In Chapter 7 we refer to Absolute Running, tiny in comparison to the Unilever giant, whose purpose of getting local people fit has made a big impact on their community.

Becoming a purpose-led organisation is not just a one-way street with benefits flowing from the company to society. As shown in the following annual letter to CEOs on reviewing 2017, Larry Fink, CEO of BlackRock, the largest global asset manager, describes a mutually beneficial exchange where potential is more likely to be realised by all stakeholders:

Society is demanding that companies, both public and private, serve a social purpose. To prosper over time, every company must not only deliver financial performance, but also show how it makes a positive contribution to society. Companies must benefit all of their stakeholders, including shareholders, employees, customers, and the communities in which they operate.

Without a sense of purpose, no company, either public or private, can achieve its full potential. It will ultimately lose the license to operate from key stakeholders. It will succumb to short-term pressures to distribute earnings, and, in the process, sacrifice investments in employee development, innovation, and capital expenditures that are necessary for long-term growth. It will remain exposed to activist campaigns that articulate a clearer goal, even if that goal serves only the shortest and narrowest of objectives. And ultimately, that company will provide subpar returns to the investors who depend on it to finance their retirement, home purchases, or higher education.[15]

If companies choose to go beyond compliance in environmental and social issues that becomes a strategic choice. Professor Ioannis Ioannou asserted during the aforementioned symposium that in recent years more effective and rigorous ESG (Environmental, Social, and Governance) data research reveals there is a positive correlation between integrating social/environmental issues into the business core and financial performance. There is a positive causal link both in the short and long term.

The correlation between purpose-led organisations and financial performance

The value of connecting to purpose may seem a paradox at face value as businesses are measured in great part by the profits they generate. Attention to anything other than the bottom line can often seem a distraction or cost. However, there are strong indicators that serving a wider purpose can be considered an investment. This investment is often expressed as the triple bottom line.

Sounds True is committed to succeeding in terms of three bottom lines: purpose, people, and profit:

We fulfil our purpose by publishing titles that inspire, support, and serve continuous spiritual awakening and its expression in the world. Fulfilling this purpose is our reason for being.

We value our people by creating a workplace that fosters authenticity, personal growth, and community.

The reward comes through evolving as individuals and caring for each other.

We create profits through working together creatively and efficiently. Optimizing our profitability enables us to re-invest capital into the business and expand our reach, making the other two bottom lines possible.[16]

Financial performance is important for all businesses to be sustainable, to be able to fulfil their purpose and continue fulfilling commitments to all stakeholders. What all the expert contributors in this chapter have in common (Simon Sinek, Professor Ioannou, Larry Fink, Sounds True) is that focusing on bigger purpose enhances rather than detracts from the bottom line. Dr Donal Collins' story can be taken as representative of this: it showed that financial benefits accrued when the business focus was altered from generating income to that of generating health outcomes.

Professor Ioannis Ioannou argues that attitudes are no longer as they were in the 1990s when analysts penalised firms for acting responsibly because of a belief in shareholder value maximisation. At that time the mindset was that socially-minded investments would necessarily decrease shareholder returns. By contrast, he asserts, the research shows now it is the perceived *gap* between the walk and the talk that analysts penalise as they recognise companies with superior responsibilities are more transparent and have more stable relationships with their stakeholders going beyond the short term resulting in more sustainable performance.[17]

In 2015, the Harvard Business Review Analytic Services team, in collaboration with the EY Beacon Institute, conducted a survey entitled the "Business Case for Purpose"[18]. In her introduction to the survey results, EY Beacon Institute global leader Valerie Keller states:

We found a very high level of consensus among these executives that purpose matters, and a widespread belief that it has positive effects on key performance drivers. The survey also demonstrates that companies who clearly articulate their purpose enjoy higher growth rates and higher levels of success in transformation and innovation initiatives.[19]

Purpose was defined in this survey as "an aspirational reason for being which inspires and provides a call to action for an organization and its partners and stakeholders and provides benefit to local and global society".[20]

The "being" that is referred to in this definition is at the core of why purpose is important. Simply put, when we are "purposeful", the way we are, our very being, is transformed. Take yourself as an example. What are the changes you notice when you know why you are doing something and that "why" agrees with your inner "why" – what you value and hold to be important? What about when you are doing something which you feel is purposeless or mindless? As you think about those two different scenarios you can probably feel the difference each one makes in your body: the difference between feeling lost, irritated and unfulfilled or engaged, inspired and committed. Which state would lead to the most productive outputs?

Research shows that high engagement amongst employees is an indicator of the highest performing organisations. Best Companies™ answers the question of what engagement is as:

When people are engaged they feel connected to each other and to the aims of the organisation they work for. They believe in a shared purpose and feel they play an important part in fulfilling it.[21]

In the 21st century we live in a world where we are more aware of our interdependence. In all spheres, environmental, economic, political and social it is apparent how shifts are no longer geographically localised. There is an underlying root system that connects us all at one point (of place or time) or another which is why we reference the importance of systemic sustainability. How organisations connect to this reality is important from executives to the wider collective of the organisation. Leaders have a duty to communicate with transparency, not leaving gaps that are quickly filled by rumour and speculation. Middle management and other individuals can also challenge a lack of connection between purposeful plans and activity. When there is a common purpose it encourages connections across as well as up and down the organisation. It means a wider accountability, regardless of role, to take responsibility for your part in the system. The greater the breadth of the conversation across the organisation to define purpose and integrate it into core activities, the greater the communication of that purpose to wider stakeholders.

ACTIVITY

Getting to Bigger Purpose

Ask yourself/yourselves one of the following questions (whichever seems most impactful) and follow the instructions from there:

? Who do we wish to become?
Once you have an answer ask

? And what's important about that?
Once you have an answer ask

? And what's important about that?
Once you have an answer ask

? And what's important about that?
Once you have an answer ask

? And what's important about that?

By now you may be thumping the table or throwing out the same answer – that's it! You've got to the most important thing!

At the beginning of this chapter we looked at core values and their close relation to purpose in indicating what is important. In the Discovery Prism©, core values answer the question "how". "How we are together" results from the conscious behaviours chosen from the values of the collective. If the values of an organisation are to be brought to life and truly reflect the experienced reality of its people and the integrity of the brand, then values need to be more than passive expressions.

What are values and why are they important?

Clarifying the value system and breathing life into it are the greatest contributions a leader can make.[22]
Peters and Waterman

Values indicate what is important to us and this can vary greatly from individual to individual, even individuals from the same family. Where values are held in common they can mean slightly different things. A husband and wife could share the value of "family" but to one it means the nuclear family and the other the extended one. Clashes could ensue. As with purpose, often our values are implicit. They are so much a part of our habitat that we don't notice they're there. We may be even hard-pressed to list which are the most important. However, whenever our values are compromised we may feel angry, upset and perhaps (if the value is deeply held) unable to function.

What does this have to do with the work environment? Everything, as values consciously or unconsciously lived are expressions of the company's culture. The way things are done relate directly to performance and results. Values are indicators of organisational culture which determines the environment which determines results.

The values an organisation actively displays are a measuring stick to its people about what's important. They tell clients and potential clients "This is what we're about, who we are, this is our identity, our brand." (The brand is the story a company tells the world about its culture; culture is the story it lives.)

Many organisations are aware of the importance of values, at least on the superficial level of pinning them to a wall, or a website. The disgraced company Enron famously listed its values as Communication, Respect and Integrity but unfortunately merely articulating those values did not mean their automatic embodiment. For real behavioural effect, pre-requisites include the collective activity of picking the values, deciding which associated behaviours result (and which are unacceptable) and putting them into action. This includes ensuring the principles relating to those values are enshrined in structures and procedures including how and who you hire, how and what you reward. Perhaps most challenging of all is the addressing of non-acceptable behaviours, wherever they appear in the organisational hierarchy.

Personal values and the organisation

But what about the people who work in the organisation – what if their values don't align with those of the company in which they work?

Imagine if the culture was "Don't question, do as you're told" wrapped in the value of loyalty yet your values were of honesty or creativity or responsibility. You'd either leave or be outwardly compliant but inwardly resentful and working at less than your potential. This is the opposite of engagement, where the person does not "show up" for work – the body is at the desk, but not much else. Conversely, the organisation would not want to hire someone who was not aligned with their values. Imagine the irony of a taciturn receptionist under a banner promising "We put the client first".

However, where there is a fit between personal values and company cultural values then the potential for engagement and performance is maximised: "In the face of turbulence and change, culture and values become the major source of continuity and coherence, of renewal and sustainability."[23]

Why choose core values?

- To stand for something
  The values espoused are a clue to a company's identity e.g. Nike's listed values are: performance, authenticity, innovation, and sustainability whilst Patagonia, also a sportswear company, does not *list* values but everything they say, do and promote is suffused with their values of sustainability, care and passion.

- To create common ground
  When values are built from the ground up (rather than as a marketing exercise), it inevitably involves people sharing ideas of what is important to them and learning about what is important to others. This positive and open exploration creates a common language which all have helped to create. This co-creation reduces assumptions and enhances understanding.

- To get alignment/focus on the same direction
  Values work is not just about deciding what is important but how what is important subsequently gets sewn into the fabric of the business. What are the behaviours stakeholders can expect as a result of these values; what are the actions in line with our values; what processes result from our values?

- To guide decision-making
  Values that are strongly held in the organisation will create a framework guiding activity. Transparently connecting values to decisions powerfully underlines the importance of that value for the organisation. For example Patagonia, who hold

deep values around sustainability, declare: "We know that our business activity – from lighting stores to dyeing shirts – creates pollution as a by-product. So we work steadily to reduce those harms. We use recycled polyester in many of our clothes and only organic, rather than pesticide-intensive, cotton".

- To agree on what's important
  Transparent and inclusive work on values is an effective method of defining and agreeing what is important to the collective.

- To inform behaviours
  Most of us know the aphorism "Honesty is the best policy" but we find not everyone has heard the continuation of that phrase "...but not the policy of an honest man". This means when honesty is truly integrated as a value then it no longer needs to be externally prompted. It is simply what the person is with no need for justification. When it comes to collective values, however, positive and negative examples of behaviour are useful as collective endorsements of what is acceptable to all stakeholders. A large health care provider placed their values on a grid showing the accompanying behaviours under the headings: *What it is* and *What it isn't*. Under the value of Team Spirit an example of *what it is* was: *Speaking up and challenging if we feel something is not right* and *what it isn't: Failing to address issues with others that have an impact on the service we provide*. We would go as far as to say if values do not inform behaviours then they hold no practical value.

- To choose the right people for the right team
  When values are integrated into the business, they will be present in the processes of recruitment. What kind of individual will be aligned with the organisation? Which questions/activities in the selection process elicit those values? There are high cost implications for hiring people

who are the wrong fit for all parties. Values-based interviews and inductions reduce the likelihood of this mismatch. Using CTT© (see below) for mergers and acquisitions can help accelerate success by addressing cultural differences at the outset.

- To identify the purpose of the group
  The close link between purpose and values was made at the beginning of this chapter. Identifying values can be a precursor to identifying purpose and vice versa. The questions: What are we about, what do we stand for, can elicit both values and purpose.

- To support change
  Values mapping (see work with CTT© below) creates a platform for change into which all have had an input and therefore buy-in is high. The wider the participation in an organisation, the greater the acceptance of required change to evolve from today to tomorrow's culture.

- To harness the power of diversity
  Talking about values lets us see what is important to people and helps understanding of differences. Understanding builds trust and trust is the basis of better working relationships. Where there is diversity, common values unite.

Values as a roadmap to cultural transformation

When we support organisations to work on their values we partner with the Barrett Values Centre (BVC) who have created metrics to make the intangible tangible. Their core purpose is expressed as follows:

We believe that organisations work better when their leaders are focused on building values-driven cultures that benefit their people, their customers and all sectors of society. We believe that when you measure your culture you can manage it.

We believe that shared values connect human beings beyond race, religion, politics, and gender. We believe that human societies grow and evolve when you reduce fear, build trust and increase love. We believe that values are powerful tools for creating a better life for ourselves and future generations. We bring passion and commitment to furthering and deepening the collective understanding of the evolution of human consciousness.[24]

Their Cultural Transformational Tools© (CTT) Cultural Values Assessment is unique in its inclusive and holistic approach to measuring culture through the values of the people of the organisation. It measures employees' personal values, the values they directly experience in the organisation, and those they wish to see. It highlights the values that the company and individuals share. It indicates the great values people want to keep, what they would like to see more of, and what is potentially blocking the company's performance. It is a tangible snapshot of the people and the organisation, a measure (which although subjective for the individual becomes objective through the weight of the collective data) of their working experience and therefore a great platform from which to explore any default behaviours which are endemic and unhelpful and conversely those which would unlock more of the organisation's potential. CTT© introduces the concept of entropy which is the amount of energy lost in the system to limiting values. This can be measured in lost revenue, employee turnover and bureaucratic processes, all of which waste energy, deplete resources and sap morale.

By contrast, alignment of values leads to greater engagement and higher performance, as BVC research has shown through mapping the values of more than 6,000 organisations in 90 different countries using the CTT©. The most successful of these organisations had either the top ten current culture values evenly spread across the Seven Levels of Organisational Consciousness© and/or had a balanced distribution of votes for all values chosen by employees across the Seven Levels of Organisational Consciousness© (see Fig. 7). Their top ten current culture values were also distributed across all segments of the Business Needs Scorecard©.[25]

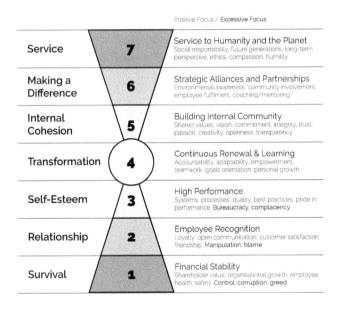

Figure 8 **Seven Levels of Organisational Consciousness (© Barrett Values Centre)**

At its core the CTT© model provides the framework to align the individual with the organisation in a way which respects both. The result is minimal loss of energy in the system and maximum energisation of the collective through consciously chosen values which reflect what's important to the population and are also reflected in behaviours which permeate the organisation. When values permeate the organisation the results are seen in the associated behaviours which are modelled by the leaders and congruent in all the systems and processes of the organisation. Since values are an expression of what is important to the population, purpose and values are inherently aligned through this activity. Unpacking the significance of values and purpose takes you a stage further towards the Prism at the centre of the framework and the energy this releases.

LIVING THE VALUES

The Global Water Partnership (GWP) is a global action network working to achieve its vision for a water secure world. It has over 3,000 partner organisations in 183 countries. A requirement for membership to the network is that partners agree to adhere to the core values which are considered paramount to pursuing its mission.

The Global Secretariat (Global Water Partnership Organisation or GWPO) is located in Stockholm, Sweden with about 25 international staff. It provides overall support and coordination to the global network in order for partners to achieve their objectives. As such it serves as a role model in how it lives its values both internally and externally, linking knowledge and resources while ensuring communication and coherence.

The wider context for GWPO as a not-for-profit organisation is a typically VUCA one (volatile, uncertain, complex and ambiguous). It faces competition for scarce resources which means competing for funding to be viable over the long term and needing to be more "performance" oriented in order to thrive, not just survive. In addition, the challenges that the organisation seeks to solve are so-called "wicked" ones where staff are required to take decisions where there is a high degree of uncertainty and ambiguity balancing the interests of multiple stakeholders. These require not just expertise and skills in the technical and knowledge areas that GWPO staff have an abundance of but also the ability to be flexible and adaptable, capable of building strong interpersonal relationships of trust with the appropriate level of accountability and courage.

GBL conducted values work with the secretariat that included two values workshops, a Barrett Values Cultural Values Assessment and meetings with the management team. The secretariat had already identified values but felt that the translation to action was lacking. They wanted to bring these to the forefront of their everyday work. The workshop sessions gave all staff the opportunity to actively contribute, deciding on values that represented them all and coming up with ways to really live these. The values chosen were transparency, collaboration, commitment and integrity. This choice was largely informed by the Cultural Values Assessment that confirmed the desire for a learning culture of trust and integrity while at the same time indicated a need for more collaboration and greater clarity in direction. Subsequent staff development work has been conducted and is ongoing to address these focus areas.

The values work at GWPO was considered to be very useful in raising awareness of what was already working and what needed more attention for it to become the strong supportive organisation it wanted and needed to be to face the challenges of performing in an increasingly difficult and complex context.

GWPO continues to reference its values in daily work. Effective reminders include values posters placed around their offices, small cards that people carry and an acknowledgement of their values at the start of meetings.

The bigger purpose and core values lens is at the apex of the Discovery Prism© framework. Purpose supplies the meaning we all seek and values are at the root of another of our deep needs, that of relating and connecting to others. When we act in alignment with both we maximise all our resources and increase our effectiveness. They are foundational to individual motivation, inspiration and engagement and yet are often given superficial consideration or completely omitted from organisational exploration. We continue the investigation of these themes from the different perspective of the overlap lenses in ongoing chapters. The overlap of this lens with vision forms the legacy lens, and we will look at vision in the next chapter.

QUESTIONS FOR REFLECTION

Bigger Purpose

? What fulfils you about working here?
? What makes you proud of your organisation?
? Why does this organisation exist?
? Who/what is your organisation in service of?
? Is there a stated purpose and how do you connect to it?

Values

? What are you most proud of?
? What are your core values (for individual and organisation)?
? How important are these values (for individual and organisation)?
? How do they show up?
? How would a third party know what your values are?
? When are your values compromised?
? What is needed for you to live your values more fully?

CHAPTER SUMMARY

Here are the main points of Chapter 2:

> Why bigger purpose and core values are in the same lens

> How trust is a by-product of knowing purpose

> The current importance of purpose-led organisations

> How extending the remit of purpose beyond the boundaries of the organisation is important for a sustainable organisation

> Correlations between purpose and financial performance

> How purpose is integral to thriving in a 21st century connected world

> The transformational properties of feeling purposeful

> How values affect how people behave and the quality of relationships

> Core values as an expression of organisational culture

> How to transform the culture of an organisation through working with core values

> The importance of alignment between individual and organisational values

CHAPTER 3

Vision

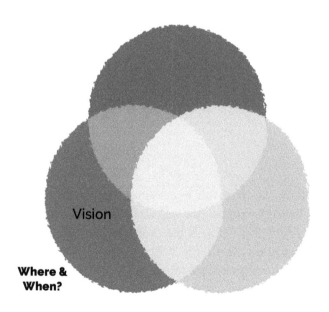

3. Vision

Without a vision the people perish.
Proverbs 29, Old Testament

In this chapter on vision we share our reflections about what is considered one of the fundamental questions of life: "Where are you going?" We encourage you to think about your destiny, as an individual, team or organisation and how your individual vision can best be aligned with a collective one.

Having a vision marks the starting point of any journey towards a desired destination. As such, it sets out our success criteria. If we don't know where we are heading, where will we get our inspiration to keep going when it's tough to do so? We define "vision" as a picture of a place in the future where we would like to be. When asked where we are heading, the words "aspirations" or "goals" may be used instead of vision. Having a vision describes a place worth reaching for. It's helpful to see this as an ideal place – you are allowed to dream!

Don't dream small dreams my friend, they have no power.
Goethe

The definition of vision is easier for some – athletes (win a gold medal), students (pass all my exams), architects (complete a building). Note the detail: not just win, but what (and where and when). Defining the vision is generally trickier for organisations. The vision may be "To be the best worldwide supplier of x" but what does that mean in concrete terms? What measures can be agreed to define "best" and what does "worldwide" mean too? And if these are not defined what happens to accountability?

Your Business will grow to match the size of your vision, fixing the vision is the biggest constraint on the scale of your future success.
Ronald Cohen[26]

The words used to describe the vision are themselves powerful. The problem with so many broadly painted visions is that they don't do the job of inciting people to put their best efforts into achieving them. They can even turn people off rather than on if they are bland and meaningless! Examples abound of meaningless vision statements, made up of fine-sounding words. These are the ones that are stated in glossy marketing brochures or on the website but rarely referenced elsewhere. If you have spent many nights in corporate hotel rooms this vision from Hilton may not resonate with you: "To fill the earth with the light and warmth of hospitality".

For a vision to be useful it needs to be connected to strategy (how we will get there), bigger purpose (our reason for being) and legacy (what we choose to leave behind). These topics will be expanded in further chapters.

Some well-formulated vision statements create a mental picture of a specific target, and are memorable and inspirational. In 1980, Bill Gates, co-founder of Microsoft, had a very clear vision – *to have a computer on every desk and in every home.* At that time Microsoft didn't produce computers and people saw little use for them, certainly not at home. Such is the change we have seen in the world since!

Setting out on a journey to reach an envisaged destination implies change as well as the consideration of what core value needs to be preserved. Crafting a vision statement is a vital early stage in any change process and one of the most cited and used change processes in business for the past few decades has been Kotter's 8-Step Process for Leading Change. Kotter refers to vision in three of those eight. Step 3 is to develop a clear, shared vision, step 4 is to communicate it and step 5 is to empower people to act on it.[27]

The ideal, whether it be ideal self, ideal team or ideal organisation, is one of the most important elements of a change cycle as, when well-defined and formulated, it will have a pull energy that acts as a magnet and inspiration.

How to create your vision

Alas! this man will never do anything, for he begins by thinking of the end of the work, before the beginning.
Pope Leo about Leonardo da Vinci

All of us have dreams and can describe a vision; it's not always realistic though. (Ask any child what they want to be when they grow up.) What is important when formulating a vision is to think about where we want to end up. The operative words here are **want** and **end**. Want is key because vision is our desired version of a great or ideal outcome. It needs to strike the balance being (even remotely) achievable without being limiting in its ambition. A good place to start is with our dreams and aspirations. It's generally easier to scale down ambition rather than reach for the stars. So once our vision starts to take some form we can still check how realistic it is.

Our vision comes from within; unless we believe in it, we can't be committed to making it happen. How likely is it that we can encourage others to join us on a journey if we don't know where we are heading and aren't really bothered whether we get there or not?

To the person who does not know where he wants to go there is no favourable wind.
Seneca, Roman statesman, philosopher

An effective way for defining a vision is the Rich Picture activity.

ACTIVITY

Rich Picture

We are all inherently creative human beings, capable of seeing our desired future and putting this, in some form, on paper. We ask participants to describe their vision as an image, first individually before pooling their ideas to create a collective one. When we announce the instructions for this activity most workshop participants will cry out that they cannot draw, no way, it wouldn't make sense to anyone, and they want to come up with words instead. Every single group we have worked with so far has come to see that the creation of an image on paper is not only more powerful in its process, but also possible, even for the greatest resistors. Pictures and symbols express so much more than words. The sighs and groans soon change to chatter and laughter and outcomes are produced that are surprising in their insightfulness. Sometimes help is needed in their interpretation, but a lot of art does these days, so there's nothing new there. In fact it is groups' interpretations of other teams' drawings that add more insights as the drawing becomes a spur to firing everyone's imagination.

A rich picture is visual but depending on our preferred type of operating or learning we may find hearing or feeling easier than seeing it. It may be a still shot or a movie playing in our heads. Ideally it is a rich experience although it may be enough to have a sketchy idea from the outset which develops in depth as steps are taken towards achieving it.

All this sounds straightforward and indeed conjuring up the picture may well be for one individual. It gets more complicated when others are involved. From an organisational point of view the vision needs to be shared by all members to be widely effective. Sharing in this sense does not just mean hitting "send to all" in an email. It's obvious that this won't work, since hearts as well as minds need to be engaged. But how do you do this? It's not always feasible to engage everyone in the organisation in a Rich Picture activity but you do want people to be on board with what the vision means, for the organisation and ultimately for themselves. People need to be inspired to work together to reach the desired future and see the point in doing so. It is amazing to note how many organisations put out their vision-mission-strategy papers without further thought, in the unquestioning expectation that people will swallow the messages whole. Other organisations assume that vision and mission are clear, without any discussion or communication.

A small business owner we know designed an away day for the first time for his company. He originally had "company goal-setting" on the agenda, but then decided that he wanted this day to be about spending fun time together away from the office. Based on his vision for the company, he penned the overall goals himself and announced them to his employees, thus missing an opportunity for his co-workers to contribute. Fun away days are important for relationship building but they are not a substitute for the buy-in to organisational identity which helping to create it brings.

People need to know there is a destination as well as a plan and have confidence that what is being aimed for is a worthwhile pursuit. Anne once asked a famous conductor how he led an orchestra when he was in the role of guest conductor. Here are highly skilled professionals who know their music, their art, but don't know their leader. The nature of their relationship and engagement is temporary, yet they are united in their short-term objective of giving a brilliant performance. No artist would risk their reputation on giving anything less (you are only as good as your last performance).

This conductor's answer displayed the essence of his leadership. He set out the vision; he knew where he was heading and orchestra members trusted him to lead them there. Anne watched him during the pre-concert rehearsal. His engaging manner instilled confidence in the orchestra members that inspired them to give their best. His reputation of course spoke for him, but it was his ability to convey in a few short hours that he could see clearly where he was heading and could take the orchestra along with him in a collaborative effort. His energy and focus in the moment combined with the certainty of achieving brilliance was palpable.

We have worked with other conductors of choirs who have done just the opposite and have experienced lacklustre performances where singers and players were not united in their efforts. Technically the performance was adequate, perhaps even excellent in parts; musically, though, it didn't inspire. Energetically you can feel the difference, whether musician or audience. When everything comes together there is a tangible buzz of energy giving an all-round positive vibe. This is the experience of attunement where the lenses overlap at the Prism, the centre of the framework.

Balancing doing with being

When formulating the vision, what is the frame of mind that is most helpful? The optimum is to define your vision with as much detail as possible using all senses. This means "being present" at the point in the future that you choose for the realisation of your vision (the "end"). So from an unstrained state of calm reflection, give yourself permission to see, feel, hear, smell and taste all that is happening in that future state. Describe all this in the present tense e.g. "I see the desks of the children in the school classrooms. This is how excited they are. This is what their teachers are saying." It may help to close your eyes to shut out distractions. It's probably easier to do this in the right context, where you feel you have the mental space. This is a creative process and it won't come to order necessarily. When asked, people say have their most creative thoughts pretty much anywhere, except at their office desk!

As far as the "end" point of the vision is concerned, different visions for different time frames and different circumstances are possible. For the conductor in the above case, it was the end of that particular performance. It may be sooner or later or even at the end of life. Our life vision should encapsulate all aspects – personal and family as well as professional dreams. Sometimes people conjure up one or the other and forget how they connect. A common regret from successful business people later in their lives is that they wish they had spent less time and effort at work and more with their loved ones. They didn't consider all stakeholders in their "system".

Vision and 21st century leadership

Why is vision crucial for good leadership? Good leaders formulate their vision and communicate it in a way that inspires others to follow them. Can you even be a leader without it? It's part of the job description – both to develop one that stands for what people in the organisation can achieve together and also to communicate it. The effect is that even in large organisations greater levels of delegation and decision-making are enabled.

There are different views about how to achieve an inspirational vision. Many scholars and practitioners argue that unless a vision reflects the aspirations of its followers in some way, it is unlikely to move people to action. Some go so far as to say that for this to happen, people should be involved in the process of creating the vision. Impossible you may say, our organisation is far too large to conduct an operation of this enormity, even if the leadership would decide it's a good idea to do so – and that's highly unlikely anyway because they are the ones who call the shots and that's what they are paid to do.

The British Heart Foundation is an example which proves such large-scale involvement is possible and can have positive long-term impact. The British Heart Foundation wanted to become a "world class organisation". In their efforts to define this vision with greater clarity, they gathered huge numbers of people across and outside of the organisation to have conversations about their vision, purpose and values. Once formulated, they recognised that people who worked there did not all see how these translated to their everyday work. The result was to create a new framework of behaviours called "Live It, Beat It". This has made a huge difference in many ways. People now engage actively with living the values, which are the subject of quarterly conversations that have replaced the annual appraisal process.

For most businesses, employees are unlikely to participate in defining the company vision, so what do we suggest instead? There are some key factors to be considered for a vision to be motivational. Firstly, leaders who formulate the vision (either on their own or together as a leadership team) need to know what it is they are striving for themselves and then they need to be aligned with fellow team members in the desired common outcomes. This is often a lot easier said than done. Peter Drucker[28] outlines four key challenges that organisations face. One of the four is this: "creating unified vision in an organisation of specialists". If this rings true for your organisation, then it's worth spending the time to form a vision collaboratively.

21ˢᵗ century leaders are those that engage others in a collaborative vision. Here's why:

- They have a very sound sense of what their people stand for, because they are connected enough to the real people issues of their company and know their ongoing challenges as well as successes.

- They do not see themselves as distanced or separated from people.

- They are good listeners and are prepared to consider some of the suggestions they hear as a result of asking for feedback from a wider circle than just their direct reports.

- They are very much in tune with external stakeholders, not least their own customer and potential customer wants and needs, now and in the future.

- They have a sense of where the market is heading because they ask the right questions and keep their heads above the day-to-day business of operations to see the wider market context and recognise developing trends.

- Knowing what key players want as well as what might emerge to create a need can then be considered alongside the capacity and will to deliver. This greater connectivity gives the vision wider appeal and relevance.

Success in any business reflects the quality of our relationships with all stakeholders. Having a clear vision that makes sense and shows a credible direction for the future is reassuring and builds trust – how else can we expect people to invest their time and efforts (our employees) and money and belief (our investors and clients)? Making sense is not the same as sensible. Bill Gates' vision made sense to him and probably would have only made sense to a few other like minds at the time. He had the vision to connect how those possibilities could affect the lives of ordinary people.

Visionary as a leadership style

When you talk to the most inspiring leaders, the kind I call successful visionaries, it turns out that they all began with passion and a view of the big picture.
Deepak Chopra[29]

Some leaders are considered "visionary". The visionary style is one of the positive styles of new leadership (as described by Daniel Goleman)[30], inspiring people to move towards shared dreams. People probably don't set out to be visionary in their style, but some just have a natural tendency to be "dreamers". As with all leadership styles it has its advantages and disadvantages, depending on the circumstances in which it comes to the fore. It is useful to be conscious of different leadership styles and what your own default may be. We encourage people to expand their range and to understand when it may be more beneficial to step back and let another leader play to her strengths in a given situation. No one leader can do it all; we are strong believers in shared leadership and in understanding what each individual can bring to the party. The StrengthsFinder 2.0 assessment is a useful tool for doing so. "Futuristic" is one of the 34 StrengthsFinder themes. This is how it is described:

People strong in the Futuristic theme are inspired by the future and what it could be. They inspire others with their visions of the future.[31]

In the Introduction chapter we talk of the "Average versus Superior Leaders" activity. In addition to observing the qualities participants assign to leaders, also noteworthy is the disparity between seeing the "visionary, inspirational" in others that participants rarely claim for themselves. This is a term reserved for the famous and legendary. The most cited are Mahatma Gandhi, Martin Luther King, Nelson Mandela and Barack Obama. All these are great statesmen of course so most (less famous) high-achieving leaders would not put themselves in the same category. If these leaders are doing their job well, they are inspiring. Great leaders create leaders of their followers. Perhaps being visionary then is not as hard as it may seem!

Sharing the vision

Having defined the vision, this must then be shared in a way that inspires others to act. At this point, many a highly competent person in a leadership role may do a double turn and disappear rapidly back where she came from. It is easy to be put off by the voice in the head that reminds us that we are not Martin Luther King and even if we have a dream we don't have the words or passion to motivate the masses.

The vision statement can be shared in many ways – not just at a large-scale gathering. It's probably most effective if shared by those who have had a part in conceiving it, preferably in person through smaller gatherings to encourage discussion. Once formulated it makes sense to test it first before going public. Ask people who will give you candid feedback whether it has the desired effect – do they feel inspired by it? Can they see their part in it? Do they feel confident that the organisation is committed to making it happen? Whether it is formulated as a sentence or a paragraph, it is useful to create a longer description that informs it – the bigger story it paints or key messages. This makes the job of testing and communicating it easier. Consider the tone: "corporate speak" is unlikely to make an emotional impact, other than derision or despair. "So many words, most of them empty" was the conclusion of a *Financial Times* journalist on being sent Microsoft's 1,500 word new mission statement in 2015[32]. A vision will be at its most powerful when connected to purpose. Relating initiatives and successes to the vision will create a clear and consistent story which reinforces it and demonstrates progress.

How the vision is useful once defined

A compelling vision statement is fundamental because it guides strategic decision-making and inspires product development, as well as the choices of whom we employ, buy from and sell to. Having a vision is only one part of the equation; anchoring that vision, communicating and delivering it are equally important. Once the vision is clear it can be referred to and provide a check against progress or necessary adjustments. Visions are not static and do shift over time.

At GBL we revisited our initial vision as we had conceived it as a brand new start-up and needed to consider how it had changed over three years. There has been some significant shift in the detail although not in the overall desire of what we wanted to achieve then and now. The shift reflected the experience and learning from running the company over this period as well as the changing ambitions of the original partners. Unless we had revisited our key positioning documents, conversations would never have happened that needed to be had. We would have continued in the assumption that we were all on the same page, which was in fact not the case.

We mention this here because we believe that a lot of the issues that all businesses face are the result of not revisiting periodically the key tenets that hold the organisation together. This is called for when the composition of the team changes, as can happen quite frequently. A key player exits and leaves a legacy that will live on and influence the changed team, for better or worse. This legacy needs noticing and addressing in order for the team to move on (see more in Chapter 7, Legacy). Poor execution is not the only reason for business failure; pursuing the wrong ideas with gusto is a common one (see Figure 16, Right vs Wrong Things Grid in Chapter 6, Strategy).

Peter Drucker, management consultant and author, asserted already in 1994: "In most cases, the right things are being done – but fruitlessly. ...The assumptions on which the organisation has been built and is being run no longer fit reality. These are the assumptions that shape any organisation's behaviour, dictate its decisions about what to do and what not to do... These assumptions are about what a company gets paid for". There are many reasons for a company to decline (either rapidly or slowly) – but it is principally because of a lack of vision or one that is outdated. In November 2014 the *Wall Street Journal*[33] reported the lack of vision of Twitter:

Twitter CEO Dick Costolo Struggles to Define Vision
Big Investors Sell Shares Amid Executive Departures,
Changing Strategy

There are ample examples in the media of similar cases for large corporates. We hear less about the millions of small businesses that suffer the same fate.

Vision alone does not suffice. We have probably all met visionary leaders who lack the ability to transfer vision to action and desired results. A leadership course participant recollected a visionary leader of a large publicly quoted company he had once worked for. This managing director was known for his grand ideas but was not terribly practical, nor particularly respected, since he spent a lot of time in his large office playing with his train set, dreaming up new plans and processes! He was a classic example of a "dreamer" (strong vision, little execution). The opposite position (strong execution, no vision) makes for a second-rate placing compared to being best at both – having a powerful vision and acting on it. As technology and business futurist Joel A. Barker said:

Vision without action is merely a dream. Action without vision just passes the time. Vision with action can change the world.

We refer to our opening citation and offer a closing quote:

"Without a vision the people perish." But, to confound Andrew Lloyd Webber and Tim Rice, not "any dream will do". Our vision must be faithful and bold, realistic and achievable, godly and honourable.

The truth of the saying is not in doubt. Any group of people that has no vision toward which they live and work – and for which they might sacrifice much – will not survive for long. It is the common purpose – the commonly held sense of direction – that holds them faithful while all around them changes.
Nick Baines, British Anglican Bishop[34]

As mentioned earlier, it is impossible to separate vision from the purpose that drives it and the strategy that brings it into being. In the following chapter on stakeholders and mission we make the connection to envisioned success – who your work is for.

VISION IN ACTION

Figure 9 **The Summit Schools, Maragua, Kenya**

In 2000, **James Ngugi** had a vision for a school in the rural district of Maragua, Kenya. Having retired as a pastor he devoted his life, along with Karen, his wife and school principal, to expand their school to accommodate 500 pupils within 5 years. Their dream was to help young people gain an education, which is the easiest route out of poverty and into a secure future. They established The Summit Schools, a primary and secondary school in the rural district of Maragua, on land that they own. The school has provided a supportive, happy and caring learning environment, where children are encouraged to pursue their talents and older students support the younger ones. In 2000, the Summit Schools provided education for about 140 pupils from the ages of five to eighteen. Those who can pay modest fees, while orphans and some others are educated for free. Numbers had risen to 220 but declined – this was partly due to the drought Kenya experienced in 2009 which meant that many parents were experiencing economic hardship and needed to withdraw their children. The school is supported by the Ngugis' small farm (shamba) which provides most of the food. The farm depends very much on adequate rainfall and crops fail in periods of drought, which means an increase in the running costs of the school. James needed help with realising his vision. Visitors to the Summit Schools, on a journey organised by the Extraordinary Leadership[35] organisation, were inspired by James and Karen's work and vision. Two practical engineers with big hearts and a strong sense of purpose saw the opportunity to solve the problem of unreliable water supply. A small group of inspired individuals set up the first borehole drilling project with funds from the WellBoring charity established to "bring clean water to African schools". Summit Schools was the first community to receive a WellBoring borehole in 2011. In 2018 WellBoring members celebrated 50 wells bringing clean water to 50 rural African schools, transforming the lives of schoolchildren, teachers and their communities. They are halfway to their updated goal of 100 wells. James' initial vision has inspired many more individuals and communities more widespread than he ever imagined. The WellBoring vision is to sustainably develop schools and communities in developing countries by providing safe, clean drinking water.

QUESTIONS FOR REFLECTION

Crafting a vision

? Where are you heading?

? Where do you want to be at some point in the future (and when)?

? What does it look like when you get there? How does that feel?

? Who is with you? What are they saying and doing?

? How will you know when you get there?

? What other overarching visions will this vision need to align with?

? How will the vision connect to your own values and that of your organisation?

? What will happen if you don't fulfil your vision?

Once you have a vision

? What is your vision (personal, team, organisational)?

? When did you last revisit your vision? Does it need adjusting or further clarity?

? How inspiring is your vision and to whom?

? How does your own vision fit with your team's (organisation's) vision?

? How connected do you feel to your team's vision?

? How long is your time horizon? (Can you work back from a long-term vision and outline a vision for a shorter timeframe that is congruent?)

? How important is your (team's) vision to your strategy and decision-making?

? Do all members of your team (organisation) have the same vision?

? Who are the important people in your life who will be affected by the fulfilment of your vision?

? How will they be affected? Is this what you and they want?

CHAPTER SUMMARY

Here are the main points of Chapter 3:

> How to define a vision and why it's important for success

> How having a vision relates to change

> The connection of vision to 21st century leadership and how a collaborative vision can be inspirational

> "Visionary" as a leadership style

> Why a vision needs to be shared and revisited periodically to be useful

> That vision alone is insufficient but must be driven by purpose and transformed into action through strategy

CHAPTER 4

Stakeholders and Mission

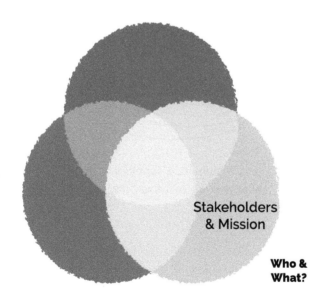

Stakeholders
& Mission

Who &
What?

4. Stakeholders and Mission

Transformational leadership is the process of collectively engaging the commitment and participation of all major stakeholder groups to radical change in the context of shared endeavour.
Peter Hawkins[36]

This chapter is about understanding whom you are here to serve, your stakeholders, and what they want and expect of you. How can you then better meet your stakeholders' needs in order to provide best value for all those you want to impact in your "system"? System is defined in the widest sense, while taking into account varying degrees of reach (people and things you can control/influence/can neither control nor influence).

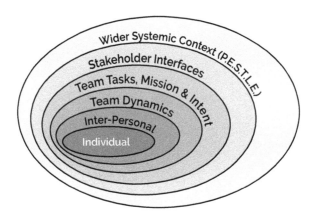

Figure 10 **System Map, supplied by AoEC**
(Academy of Executive Coaching)

Mission

The mission question is about what you do, what business you are in. What do you provide of value in order to meet your client needs? And what are you uniquely placed to do that no other person or team or organisation can? Mission is defined as an assignment, or something to be fulfilled. It is often described as a journey with a beginning and end and should link to "bigger purpose" (this has been defined in Chapter 3). The terms "mission" and "purpose" are sometimes interchanged. Many companies call their mission what we would call "bigger purpose". What matters is consistent usage, the common language used within the organisation.

Here's an example from NASA:

> *The Mars 2020 rover mission is part of NASA's Mars Exploration Program, a long-term effort of robotic exploration of the Red Planet. The Mars 2020 mission addresses high-priority science goals for Mars exploration, including key questions about the potential for life on Mars. The mission takes the next step by not only seeking signs of habitable conditions on Mars in the ancient past, but also searching for signs of past microbial life itself.*[37]

The big purpose here is to understand the potential for life on Mars envisioning human existence at some far distant point on this planet. NASA is in the business of operating missions to discover the facts (the robotic exploration of the Red Planet) – in business terms they are doing the feasibility studies.

A useful way of formulating company mission is to start with "We are in the business of..."

GBL's mission: We're in the business of people development. People learn to connect the why, the what and the how and so produce extraordinary results.

The definition may not be as easy as it seems. Since clarity is critical for providing focus for staff as well as management, it's worth spending some time to make sure there is agreement about how you define your business and to keep revisiting this periodically. Reaffirming the answers to the "big questions" needs constant repetition to maintain awareness and keep relevant. There is a direct link between clarity and organisational success. On the subject of organisation health, which management thought leader Patrick Lencioni describes as the "one remaining, untapped competitive advantage", the key focus is clarity and having a cohesive leadership team.[38]

Once clear about the business you are in it is easier to consider what is needed to satisfy your stakeholder requirements and manage or exceed their expectations. It is also here that connections will be made to bigger purpose, vision and strategy. Some organisations have strategic business planning documents that have already been developed (e.g. business plan, business scorecard) without being clear about the answers to the big questions. If this is the case, spending time to review the alignment between all the lenses is worthwhile to avoid the repercussions of any disconnect. A useful metaphor is that of a zoom camera lens where you keep switching from the wide angle to the micro view and back again. You can't be crystal clear about all views simultaneously, but it is counterproductive to assume clarity without first checking. Mission and stakeholders are together in the same lens because you cannot have one without the other. Considering them in the light of each other can bring fresh insights. It's unlikely that when you think through and talk about the business you are in you will not consider whom your product or service is for. Most readers will already have defined both, so it will be a more useful exercise to think through your current status and where you aspire to be, how viable your business is considering future trends and to check consistency with all other lenses. The simple act of reflection may uncover some gaps or confirm that all is aligned.

Here's a mission statement from Morning Star, the world's largest tomato processing company. (It processes 40% of California's processed tomato crop.) Morning Star is an example of a very large successful company that is often singled out as a role model for its embodiment of self-management principles and as an example of 21st century management practices. It is a "teal organisation" in Laloux's terms[39]. Later in this chapter we look at this concept in more detail.

> *Our Mission is to produce tomato products and services which consistently achieve the quality and service expectations of our customers in a cost effective, environmentally responsible manner. We will provide bulk-packaged products to food processors and customer-branded, finished products to the food service and retail trade.[40]*

The following mission is from Neo, a small British communications agency on the journey towards becoming "teal".

> *What we do: Tell the stories that matter*

> *It's your stories that count. Your work. Your ambitions. Our work is about making this matter more. We build brands. We create campaigns. We design and write communications. We do so with creativity, objectivity and a belief that the best stories should belong to those that are changing the world for the better.[41]*

In a leadership development workshop Anne was discussing mission and stakeholders with participants and encouraging them to be clear about whom they serve. A participant was quite convinced that his job was not to serve anyone; he was not a manager, just a team member of a project team that "only" provided information for internal use. He failed to see the connection between the hours he put in at work and how this impacted anyone else in his own organisation. What convinced him otherwise was the question "Who appreciates the work you do and would miss you if you were away for some time?" He left with a clearer understanding of his own contribution towards team and overall company effort. Understanding contribution and impact on others makes a real difference to people because it provides meaning. Ideally we want to know that our endeavours are meaningful, not just for ourselves but for others too.

Why is it important to answer "what we are doing" and "for whom"?

Clarity of focus is essential, today more than ever, because we are bombarded with so much information from so many sources on a daily basis that it is easy to "get bogged down", make unconscious choices based on our own preferences or run off in different directions. This can take us away from our grounded being. In taking a step back on a regular basis and reminding ourselves of our priorities, who we are as well as what we do, we can better serve those whom we consider to be of prime concern. We keep asking the question "Whom are we here to serve?"

Conducting an analysis of our stakeholder groups (by mapping or other techniques) enables us to see our place in the wider system and the connections between different stakeholder groups. The reach of the stakeholder net can be consciously decided – has anyone been left out? Without understanding who our stakeholders are, their needs, expectations and requests, it is impossible to gauge how we are fulfilling them currently and what more we should be doing to manage expectations and perform to our full potential. We may uncover some gaps in our service, even some uncomfortable truths that are better to address sooner rather than later.

In defining or re-evaluating our mission and key stakeholders we may conclude that our business focus is too narrow or wide, or that critical members of our team are pulling in different directions because they had a different understanding of either or both!

Stakeholders

The stakeholder link to business performance

The old view was that business performance should be measured in purely financial terms, the holy grail being the maximisation of shareholder value. There is now mounting evidence to refute this as the only measure of success for companies. In fact, companies that are considered "responsible" outperform both in the short and long term. They have a positive sociological impact on the diverse constituencies that they serve. These companies reward stakeholders both by financial as well as non-financial means, they invest in meaningful stakeholder relationships, and are transparent and accountable e.g. by measuring their impact and disclosing it. They are more likely to choose partners like them so responsibility extends to their partners in the supply chain.

How organisations are led successfully has evolved over centuries and continues to do so. What was in vogue in the 19th century (hierarchies and formal roles that separated the decision-makers from the action-takers) was no longer considered the most effective way to run a business in the 20th century (typically with a focus on profit and growth and management by objectives). In today's world of work there has been a noticeable shift in attitude towards a preference for more collaboration, shared decision-making and the questioning of growth for growth's sake without concern for the planet's overstretched resources. Organisations that reflect this thinking invest in organisational culture, values and empowerment to boost employee engagement. All these management modes are to be found in our current business landscape, some more prevalent than others depending on the industry or type (whether private, public or not for profit). The evolution of organisations is "teal" as described by Frederic Laloux[42] and takes a whole systems view of a business, looking at its purpose to serve a multitude of stakeholders. A few organisations of this type exist (including Neo and Morning Star, mentioned above) and many leadership scholars and practitioners today consider that they are modelling the next stage in evolutionary shift.

In the Strategy chapter we describe "teal organisations" in more detail. Why do you need to know all this? We believe that it depends a great deal on the type of organisation that you work for as to how stakeholders are viewed, valued and treated. In the chapter on promises, we elaborate on this topic.

The following outlines a process to define key stakeholders. It is not intended as a full and detailed description but rather to help you choose the questions most useful for your specific context. You might note that this linear process does not seem to fit with "emergence principles" that are called for in 21st century organisations. What is key is the facilitation of such a process and the spirit in which it is conducted to promote true listening and dialogue.

Stakeholder engagement process

Clarify desired outcomes

At the start of any process be clear about the purpose of the enquiry and level of ambition. What are you doing now, and what have you done before to engage with stakeholders? What do you want to achieve (e.g. to run a health check, to be more transparent, to modify your communications, to improve your relationships and performance, to engage in a transformative journey)? What new influencers do you wish to attract (e.g. who are looking for a match in values with their suppliers)? What are your desired outcomes (your vision for this work)? What are your available resources and your limitations given your current context?

Stakeholder mapping

Once the purpose of your enquiry is clear you need to understand who your stakeholders are. Who has a stake or an interest in your business? Since sustainability in the 21st century is about increasing the net, it's practical to start by considering those stakeholders who are not so obvious and perhaps impact your business even in a small way e.g. wider business community, social groups, the environment. The obvious stakeholders are your clients, shareholders, suppliers, competition, employees and their families. Stakeholders may not be in the classic positions of formal authority but can be people with high influence who are well connected. In our global interconnected world there are private companies that are larger than states – their "constituents" can come from all walks of life and from almost any country on the planet, so the responsibility that goes along with catering to their needs is an enormous one. The boundaries between business and government have become blurred.

> *Increasingly, financial markets are becoming political markets. That requires different skills – skills not all of us have acquired at university; how to properly deal with society, for example, a stakeholder that has immensely grown in importance since the financial crisis.*
> Josef Ackermann, formerly of Deutsche Bank[43]

Prioritising stakeholders

Having defined all your stakeholders you can then rank them in order of priority. One way of doing this is to use a widely known model: the Influence and Interest Grid.[44]

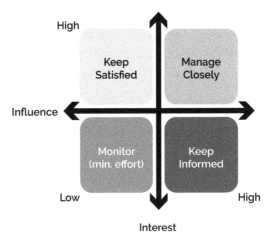

Figure 11 **Interest and Influence Grid**

At GBL we have come up with a different grid that is more aligned with our bigger purpose. In the end it is our ambition to find the best match of our services to our clients – that enables us to fulfil our purpose. We propose the following: the Values Match and Readiness Grid.

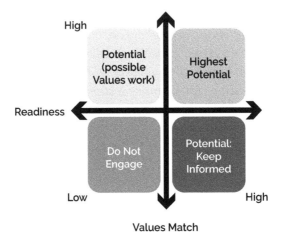

Figure 12 **Values Match and Readiness Grid**

If a team or organisation is ready, willing and able to engage in development work and the presenting (or desired) values are a close match to our own, then we have the highest potential to add value by supporting them. So in deciding "best match" we are interested in exploring their vision for development and whether that vision is something that could be achieved through our co-creation with them.

To reiterate some key points about the 21st century organisation, if work is no longer to be merely a place where we put in the hours to earn a living, but a community where we can fulfil our potential and make a meaningful contribution, then as individuals we need to seek the highest alignment of what we offer to what our employer or our client is seeking and values. We can all deliver work of "good enough" standard in a whole range of areas, but unless we are working in our sweet spot for some of the time we are not making best use of our energies and at worst even depleting our limited resources. Gartner recently reported the key trends and implications for work in 2027. One of the planning assumptions is that we will work not just for money but for passion and purpose.

> *Our impact and value will be tied to our mission, our purpose and our passion. Businesses and institutions will make themselves attractive not solely by money, but by offering us an opportunity to fuel our purpose and make a socially meaningful impact through work.*[45]

Once you have decided on a ranking for your individual stakeholders or stakeholder groups you should then consider whether this ranking would still hold under changing circumstances. Also think about the overall balance i.e. the impact of your concentrated efforts towards key stakeholders on others you have identified. A common source of failure is the over-emphasis of one or another group that adversely affects others e.g. shareholders get primacy while customers, employees and community are squeezed. This position is not sustainable and seems to be more acknowledged than ever before. One of our clients, a large global organisation, shared that they had been focused on following the lead of their largest competitor even though doing so adversely affected their own clients. It took an irate call from an influential client to re-address their priorities. We are however warned that the old "client is king" adage is not necessarily the best:

> *Clients do not come first. Employees come first. If you take care of your employees, they will take care of the clients.*
> Richard Branson

ENGAGING WITH STAKEHOLDERS

A new MD was engaged on a visit with a past client with the potential to become a large client again if the relationship could be rekindled. At first it seemed the reason the manager had agreed to see her was to rail against a previous distributor who had sold her products a decade since. The tirade ended in the accusation "Your products are s**t!" The MD didn't flinch or try to defend but asked the question "When did you last buy one of these products?" "Ten years ago, and never since." The MD then asked, "The products you're now buying, do you remember what they were like 10 years ago?" "Things have come a long way since then," the former client replied. "Could you imagine that ours have too?" the MD stated simply. The conversation shifted to a new footing that led in time to new orders being placed.

Understanding stakeholder expectations

Asking for feedback

You can understand stakeholder expectations by asking stakeholders for their feedback. How you do this will be determined by the number of stakeholders you have identified (ask a representative sample if there are many) and how you are connected to them. You may have very disparate groups that you don't have regular contact with or that represent large numbers of people, in which case you will probably run an online questionnaire. The alternative is to speak to your stakeholders in person. In all cases the higher the quality of the connection to the stakeholders, the more accurate the feedback.

Questionnaires

Standard surveys and questionnaires mostly focus on gathering "hard data" and usually don't seek to give a temperature check on emotion. We know that people, regardless of which stakeholder category they belong to, are to a greater or lesser extent governed by their emotions. It is not the technical specifications or the price that decide the sale, nor the attraction of better benefits elsewhere that are the deciding factor for your best employees to leave. Understanding the emotional factors at work is key to getting the full picture. It is equally important to understand what stakeholders **don't** want – failing to discover this is the failing of many relationships!

Stakeholder meetings

We have asked for face to face feedback ourselves and have encouraged lots of our workshop participants to do the same. The more you value your stakeholders' opinions and the closer the relationship you have with them, the more daunting it is to ask. There is vulnerability in asking for an evaluation that may be positive (which of course we would love to hear) but also critical and discouraging (that we may prefer not to know if we take this personally). However, if the intention is honest improvement then feedback is invaluable. Select your interviewees carefully – they should be respected respondents interested in your individual or collective progress.

For leaders new to an organisation, a wise practice is to conduct meetings with a range of stakeholders inside and outside the organisation. This is nothing new, but what may be is the spirit in which the meeting is conducted, with the intention of honouring the person invited and the contribution and insights they bring.

One such encounter came from an organisation at an interim stage. The current head had recently left while the newly appointed head was in the early stages of on-boarding. Our client, who had a senior role in the organisation, had been summoned to meet the new head. She had been in a state of anxious anticipation (assuming that her job might be on the line) and had found out to her great surprise that the purpose of the meeting was "to get to know her and hear her input and insights". In all her professional career, she had never been asked this before and was excited by the prospect that her new head was interested in her views and may even be keen to take them into consideration.

When conducted in a more formal, structured way, such meetings are called Listening Tours and commonly practised by new incumbents to a senior role.[46]

> *Even though I had been here a long time, it wasn't until I started to talk to people that I really learned what they actually thought. Make sure you begin to unpack the old issues, and spend time with your internal customers talking about what's working and what's not working. Like all things, it's always a two-way street.*

HOW NOT TO DO IT: THE NEW VP

"The biggest block to progress is legacy staff!"

This was the declaration from our interviewee (who prefers to remain anonymous) from his new Vice President on starting her role in the organisation, a major British infrastructure group. The new VP is a complete industry outsider and started her tenure by bringing in external consultants (who have been paid "inordinate sums of money") to draw up plans for the new way the company should be run. Showing a lack of regard for the experience of her direct reports gained over decades in the industry, this VP is of the firm belief that "legacy staff" are of no value and in fact to be seen as blockers to necessary change. The incumbent directors were required to apply for half the available roles in the new organisation. Our interviewee didn't get past the baseline test (the precursor to applying for his own job), conducted by an external consultant who treated his subjects "like schoolchildren preparing for an exam". The case examples presented on which the evaluation was based were not industry related and were of no relevance to their role or experience. The interviewee lamented the VP's starting approach as the opposite to what he would have done in the same position – i.e. to ask people what was good and working and what their suggestions for improvement would be.

In the meeting where our interviewee was told that he hadn't done well enough in the assessment to go forward to the next stage, he asked what his options were. The top tier management present slid an envelope across the table and said that they had prepared an offer for him to leave. Since he was interested in keeping his job he declined to open it and pressed for other options. He is still in the organisation, has no respect for any of his new management team, and is counting the days until he can retire.

Why does he stay? To manage his team and make sure they can do their jobs to the best of their ability and as well as he can secure for them. He considers them "more vulnerable" since they still have school-age children, mortgages to pay and low prospects of getting other jobs in the current difficult economic climate. Over the medium term he is working on negotiating a satisfactory exit.

What is the mindset needed to ask for feedback?

When asking for any kind of feedback, we encourage an attitude of humble enquiry. This means to come from a place of interest and curiosity, seeking to understand in order to uncover any unknown truths. Although there may be a strong compulsion to justify, react defensively or to feed back negatively that seems critical or even hurtful, it is counterproductive to do so and will undermine the relationship.

At times and with certain people this may be easier said than done and requires some courage and resilience. It helps to remember that without hearing various versions of "the truth" as others see it, we will not be able to become more of who we are and truly want to be.

Practise first on easier cases to develop your genuine enquiry and open listening skills before tackling the trickier ones!

Analysing the feedback

Allow adequate time for this; you may need more than one session if the results are detailed and the reports lengthy. Having conducted the information gathering there is no point rushing to come to quick conclusions and action plans. The work is much more nuanced than that. Consider including as many people as you can in the activity. The purpose is to define the main areas of attention from all the input that are most significant for your ongoing performance and development. You want to uncover the gaps between how you expected your stakeholders to rate you and how they did. This can also be a two-way process, in which case you will also need to have defined your collective expectations of them and how they are performing against these. You can revisit your chosen grid to reposition some of the dots and become clearer about who your strongest supporters are as well as the biggest blockers to your own progress. You may notice some unexpected connections e.g. where different stakeholders impact each other. Perhaps you will discover new "best match candidates" for what you are offering. Once you have the key findings think about how these are connected to your purpose and values. How would your mission shift if you were to act upon new requests? Who would you need to be, and what would you have to do in order to meet all expectations? What is realistic?

In our grid example, the boxes now look like this:

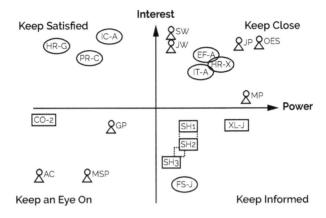

Figure 13 **Example of a Stakeholder Map**

Some useful questions at this stage:

- What unanswered questions do you still want input on?

- What is the nature of the respective stakeholder's interest in your work (e.g. financial, emotional, historical) as well as how negative or positive it may be?

- What motivates your different stakeholders most of all?

- Who else may influence their opinions generally and of you? (This enquiry can uncover some other stakeholders that haven't been in your field of vision so far.)

- How will you deal with critical feedback that you consider unfair, unjust or outside your scope of influence and control?

- Who is best positioned to conduct the stakeholder interviews? (This may be a team member for each contact, or a third party who conducts all interviews.)

ACTIVITY

An Example of Stakeholder Analysis Using Team Connect 360[47]

Team Connect 360 is an online tool that provides feedback both from internal as well as external stakeholders, giving a clear picture of how well the team is connected within its organisational system and what it can do to be more effective. It reports on stakeholder expectations and relationships with the team as well as on internal team relationships, tasks and the capacity to deliver.

Once the team has chosen its stakeholders and the online feedback process is complete, the team meets to study the report and make sense of the findings. We look for confirmation of what was known or assumed and surprises. We consider what further exploration is needed and how this can be conducted. Usually this takes the form of a dialogue with chosen individuals or groups. Team members thank their respondents for taking the time to complete the questionnaire and commit to communicating key findings and outcomes as appropriate.

Our experience with this kind of tool has been overwhelmingly positive – team members are able to gather a lot of useful and detailed information from many sources with very little effort, representing time and resources well spent. The dialogue between team members when debriefing on the questionnaire is found to be very valuable. People are keen to understand more e.g. to clarify the extent of their influence and control and to define specific, observable measures for "improvement". The discovery process as a team can help team members to focus more on the team as a whole and less on their individual agenda.

The limitations of stakeholder questionnaires

What can happen when running surveys, typically for internal stakeholder groups like the employee engagement ones, is that you find confirmation enough for what you are seeking (positive affirmation) and ignore what would be really useful in understanding more because it is potentially negative and may prove inconvenient. As much as we would like, we are all biased, whether consciously or not. We need to be prepared to practice genuine enquiry and open listening to get the true value from the results.

As with any questionnaire of this kind there are always limitations that need to be recognised. Be clear about your intentions when asking for feedback – if you don't intend to act on it, there is little point in conducting it.

Questionnaires remove bias to some extent because the same questions are being asked of all raters in an impersonal way, but the choice of questions is set and may not match exactly the questions you would prefer to ask.

Time is of the essence. Anne worked with a team that would have benefited from conducting stakeholder enquiry at the beginning of the engagement but found they were at a critical stage in their development and may not have coped with the extra effort involved in switching their focus. The timing of the enquiry is not only important for the team but also for their raters – since more people are being asked to give feedback constantly, either in person or online, they are less inclined to want to do so, even if it is for their own benefit in the long run. Assessment saturation is noticeable in some organisations, and particularly at certain points in the year, so asking for any input would not produce sufficiently meaningful results.

Barry Oshry's work[48] is another source for understanding stakeholder perspectives. Oshry proposes that we can change "system blindness" into "system sight". The nature of organisations (or "the system") is such that challenges are inherent. Issues may be interpreted as personal when they're not. We make up stories to explain our truth, yet there is a consistent pattern. The accountable "tops" (company management) are frequently overwhelmed with the complexity of their task, the "middles" are stretched and squeezed and the "bottoms" are misrepresented, vulnerable and feel unfairly treated. Neglected customers and suppliers also come into the picture in order to understand the whole system. By raising awareness of patterns that are repeated, and by taking responsibility for our own position, Oshry maintains that we are able to step into leadership, whatever our role, and live and work together in productive partnership.

ACTIVITY

Stakeholder Mapping and Feedback

This exercise serves to raise awareness of performance related to stakeholder groups and to put an action plan into place to bridge the gap between current levels and ideal.

- Encourage each member of the team to think of their range of stakeholders. This includes team members, the team as an entity, other teams within the organisation, the organisation, clients, potential clients and others depending on the industry e.g. regulators, community, new hires etc. Make the net as wide as possible.

- Without defining any further parameters split the team into small groups working on two or three of the defined stakeholders. The remit is to envision what a score of 10/10 (level of service/engagement where 1 = poorest and 10 = ideal) would look like from each of the stakeholders. What would be happening? What would the impact be?

- The team then scores themselves on a scale from 1–10 on how they feel they are fulfilling their mission for each of the stakeholders.

- Open up discussion across the groups so there is input on all stakeholders from all of the team.

- Conclude with suggestions for and commitment to actions to bridge the gap between the current score and the ideal. When self-scoring in a safe space where people can speak openly, a team will be rigorous in holding themselves to account.

Managing stakeholder relationships

The term commonly used is "managing stakeholders", yet we want to sound a warning bell. You can manage a relationship or stakeholder expectations but not another person or group of people whoever they may be. You may seek to influence others but will rarely have direct control. This is a redundant mindset in 21st century leadership.

Managing the relationship means connecting with people important to you and your business and developing the relationship in the way that best matches your intentions. You will need to set boundaries, ideally at the beginning of the engagement with your key stakeholders. Their wishes may not be realistic. If you can't provide what they are looking for, are you the right choice for them? What other options do you or they have to satisfy their needs?

In the real world, messages get mixed and much dissatisfaction is caused by misunderstandings. The clearer we can be in our communication of expectations and intentions, the better the relationship is likely to be. Balancing the needs and "need to know" of our different stakeholder groups and insisting on the correct order of making sensitive information public is imperative. There are many examples when the press has reported significant changes about companies (share reallocation, funding issues, reshuffling of senior executives, mass dismissals) before those most affected have been informed themselves. The negative impact is incalculable.

In conclusion, we refer to "stakeholder management" as a process that needs to be conducted in a systematic, ongoing way, while focusing on the essence, summed up in a quote from a senior marketing professional from the rail transport industry:

> *The (stakeholder management) process is really about the hygiene factors... sure it needs to be understood, tracked and 'managed' as a process, but in the end what makes all the difference is the quality of the relationship. An ability to ask the right questions, to listen and to engage on an emotional level. Process is task. What counts is emotional intelligence.*

As a conclusion to this chapter we come back to the central tenet, in the words of Abdul to a despairing Queen Victoria, nearing the end of her life (from the film *Victoria and Abdul*).

> *What is the point Abdul, what is the point?*

> *Service, madam. We are not here to worry about ourselves, we are here for a greater purpose.*

QUESTIONS FOR REFLECTION

Mission Questions

? What is the work you do?

? What is your "joint endeavour" – what are your team's specific objectives?

? What is unique about your work that only you can accomplish?

? What are the critical few things this team does that make the biggest difference to the business?

? What does achieving your joint endeavour make possible for your stakeholders?

? What are your roles?

? How clear are you about the roles of others on your team or in your organisation?

Stakeholder Questions

? Who are your team's stakeholders?

? What are their expectations in terms of results?

? How do you measure these?

? How well do you serve them currently?

? What is the level of service you provide?

? How connected do you feel to your stakeholders? What gets in the way?

? What needs to be different?

? What do you contribute to or co-create with your stakeholders?

? What are the stakeholders requiring that is different from organisational needs?

? What is in the wider context that impacts your business?

? If we didn't exist who would miss us?

? How can taking the position of our key stakeholder(s) help us to see the future more clearly?

CHAPTER SUMMARY

Here are the main points of Chapter 4:

- Understanding who you serve (the reason for our existence) i.e. your stakeholders

- Knowing how wide to draw the net and how to prioritise your stakeholders (who may you decide not to serve, when you consider your bigger purpose and vision?)

- Finding out what your key stakeholder expectations are and how to manage them

- Understanding how well you serve your stakeholders and how you may improve your service

- Defining the business you are in – what is it you do and what is changing? Do you need to consider significant changes caused by a threat to your current business (that can come from practically anywhere today)?

- By thinking through the questions and doing the work you should be able to answer the question: what is our value and to whom? What greater value can we provide?

CHAPTER 5

Promises

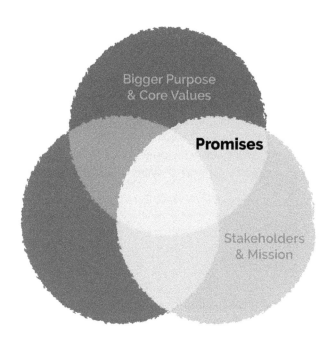

5. Promises

Your employees are the face of your brand and representatives of your company's culture. How they interact, think, operate and work together should be in line with what you promise to your customers. When your Internal and External Brand work in synch – good things happen.[49]

Promises is the lens formed at the intersection between stakeholders and mission and core values and bigger purpose. This overlap looks at two kinds of promises – those made to our internal stakeholders (organisational culture) and those made to our external stakeholders (our brand). To be authentic and create a thriving, sustainable organisation we need to match internal to external promises. Before the advent of digital mass communication with access to constant online connection a company may have survived despite a disconnect between the culture and the brand. It was never the ideal and it is certainly no longer the case in the 21ˢᵗ century when transparency, authenticity and congruence are highly visible to stakeholders.

In this chapter we look at culture and brand first as separate entities before drawing conclusions about how they need to interlink seamlessly to support thriving, sustainable 21ˢᵗ century organisations.

Culture

Culture is how the organisation is lived on the inside. It's the sum of what people think, feel, expect and believe which is reflected by how they behave. Since people mostly want to fit in they behave in compliance with the norms and rules of the group. It's easily summed up as "how we do things around here". In other words, culture is just a collective term for how the majority of people in any grouping behave. Culture can relate to countries, regions, generations, professions, ethnic groups as well as organisations.

Figure 14 **The Culture Tree**

The tangibles and the intangibles

The tree is a useful symbol to understand culture. There's a visible, tangible part, above the ground **and** a whole set of intangible qualities and attributes that make an organisation distinctive. The visible tangibles relate to our senses – everything we see, hear, touch, taste or smell. We form an impression based on what we experience. The intangibles are the not so obvious, often unconscious assumptions, expectations, values, beliefs and norms. Our idea of how best to lead a team, the right way to conduct business in a "polite and professional manner", what is an "on-time" or "late" delivery, may all be interpreted in very different ways depending on the culture.

Culture change

Culture is not static and shifts over time, in fact it needs to adapt to the ongoing changes of the environment in order to thrive. The problem with "culture" is that is often talked about but poorly defined. It's not obvious to many people that they form an intrinsic part of it and that culture is just a reflection of how they act on a daily basis. We know that behaviour is driven by what people believe and assume to be true, but there are many versions of "the truth". We are creatures of comfort who prefer the company of others who are similar to us. There are plenty of benefits of sticking together (safety, strength in numbers, bigger clout etc.) but a logical extension for some of keeping the group safe is to rigidly delimit the in-group and the out-group so the culture is not open to anything that doesn't fit with its preferred version of the truth. People generally find it difficult to stretch to embrace change because it's uncomfortable. They don't want to rock the status quo and can always find plenty of examples of why they shouldn't change their thinking or relationships or practices and so gravitate to people who will back them in their efforts to resist change. Typical cries of protest that are played out in so many scenarios in homes, schools, offices, governments are, "It has worked for us so far, why would we change?", "We can't have these outsiders coming in and telling us what to do!" and "No point in engaging in this initiative – it didn't work last time so why would it now?"

What needs to happen to embrace and benefit from difference and change, since we can't stop it but can choose how we encounter it? It starts with having a solid foundation, enough "safety" from which to venture out of our comfort zones. This solid base comes from supportive trusting relationships, enough security and a sense of "home" to which we belong although the world around us is changing.

Next, we need acceptance of what is, and attributes such as daring, curiosity, openness to new thinking, resilience and flexibility.

These are easy to say and harder to be! The catalyst for change in the end often comes down to understanding how it will benefit the individual (over the short or longer term) or because current circumstances are so bad that not changing is not an option.

What needs to happen more in organisations is having conversations that question (subconscious) beliefs and assumptions and understanding how our values influence the kind of culture we need to succeed. We notice that people sometimes know what the values of the organisation are because they have seen them on a poster somewhere but struggle to recall the words. They are often unable to relate how their own actions and their experience of others' behaviours towards each other connect to stated corporate values and beliefs. They often don't realise their own daily contribution to organisation culture with the choices they make, consciously or unconsciously. We believe that raising awareness of what people choose to believe and think can help them make conscious choices about their outcomes. A much-quoted citation from Mahatma Gandhi is a useful mantra:

Your beliefs become your thoughts, your thoughts become your words, your words become your actions, your actions become your habits, your habits become your values, your values become your destiny.

An HR manager in a large organisation had run "values" training for all staff to tell them what their values were (or were supposed to be) in order to make people comply to a desired company norm. She was embarrassed to have been part of this in her HR role, but the values had been dictated by upper management and at the time their Head of HR had believed it was the right thing to do to make their organisational culture powerful. People are unlikely to engage with company promises when their experience is that these are broken e.g. the stated value is "teamwork and collaboration" but individual targets are rewarded. As a result of the car emissions scandal Volkswagen have understood the need for a radical culture change and have redrafted their values with the help of their 11,000 employees. They knew they had to make new promises to draw a line under the scandal and have the possibility of a new start.

Brand promises

The brand is the story an organisation tells the outside world about who it is. Brand wields a power in our lives that we don't often recognise. It informs our choices about what to buy, where to live, who to be associated with and which company to work for. We may not like the idea of "personal branding" but in essence our reputation – how we are perceived by others – is something we cannot avoid, and a whole industry exists around defining and marketing your personal brand, seeing this as a cornerstone to individual and professional success. In a similar way the employer brand has received increasing attention by organisations that are keen to attract the calibre of talent that best meets their needs.

The employer brand has been described as "a set of attributes and qualities – often intangible – that makes an organisation distinctive, promises a particular kind of employment experience and appeals to those people who will thrive and perform best in its culture".[50] Employer branding is growing in importance because of the global war for talent and the recognition that it makes sense to recruit people who will fit in well to organisational culture. (Corporate brand in contrast is more general, describing the organisation's reputation and value proposition to its customers). Getting the right talent in the door and retaining the best people means huge cost savings. When people can "bring themselves to work" i.e. who they are is aligned with the culture of the organisation, they are most likely to be happy and engaged employees. High employee engagement has a direct impact on the bottom line, as numerous studies indicate. In addition, we know that employee indifference is a main cause of customer defections to other brands. Clients today are more discerning about who they buy from. The choice is less about product and more about what the organisation stands for and how they are treated by it.

So regardless of the size of your organisation, it makes business sense to consider and deliver on your promises. Most importantly brand can no longer be regarded as an entity separate from culture, because brand is defined *through* culture or the countless ways your people represent your organisation inside and outside of it.

It is common practice for larger organisations to work with external partners (brand agencies) to design, create and display their brand image with the aim of making them more powerfully visible to the outside world. Greater visibility and recognition is correlated to being a trusted supplier and thus bring higher sales and returns. In today's world and in the wake of many corporate disgraces this equation no longer adds up. One noteworthy example is Facebook which is still trying to mend its damaged reputation following the Cambridge Analytica scandal that struck in March 2018.

To recover from damage to a company's reputation, promises need restating and renewing. For Facebook this meant a public apology for the breach of trust:

> *We have a responsibility to protect your information. If we can't, we don't deserve it.*
> Full-page ads published in a number of UK and US newspapers

"Rebranding" is also conducted when a company wants to change its name, there is a change of ownership (e.g. generation shift, mergers and acquisitions and fusions), or to reflect significant changes in the customer or market landscape. The intention is to support a new all-round look and feel, to build the kind of relationships with the stakeholders that will enable the company's needs to thrive. The brand is conveyed through multiple means, tangible and intangible. Tangible methods include signage, print materials, office décor and digital media presence. Enlightened managers understand that the job cannot be done by tangible means alone. Painting the walls purple and installing the smart new furniture in the lobby, staff canteen and meeting rooms may highlight a change to something more new and dynamic, but as long as employees lack conviction and are not motivated to approach their work and their clients in a more positive, dynamic and uplifting way, the new branding will be unlikely to bring the desired rewards. It is not yet common knowledge, but many more organisations are becoming aware that you can't build a great brand without considering both the tree and its roots and how it contributes to a whole ecosystem.

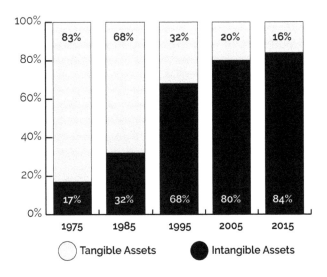

Figure 15 **Components of S&P Market Value (used with permission)**[51]

This graph shows the increasing proportion of intangible assets to market value over time. Every point of contact from the inside to outside the organisation must be considered, whether experienced live (e.g. through a sales visit or customer service call) or virtually (including online chat responses to customer queries and social media presence). What counts is the lasting impression of the client experience when in contact with the organisation. However carefully messaging is crafted and delivered, the unintended consequences of a poor experience cannot be underestimated. We all know how it makes us feel to wait in a long phone queue to reach customer support, to be passed from one person to another, to repeat our story, to not get the desired reply, to be treated with a lack of respect, to not receive a response at all to a request, or to wait for an unreasonable length of time to hear back about a matter that is of high importance to us. It's the feeling that counts! Dissatisfaction, frustration and helplessness all contribute to the lasting impression we take away from an interaction and over time cause us to remove our custom.

The role of trust

As highlighted in the Facebook example above, we trust those who deliver on their promises.

The Edelman Trust Barometer tracks trust in nations across the world over time and the most recent trend shows an alarming decrease in how trustworthy government and businesses are perceived as being in the vast majority of countries. The Global Report headline for 2017 was "Trust in Crisis" and for 2018 "The Battle for Truth". Nearly 7 in 10 people across the world worry about fake news as a weapon. In 2018 a 42% loss of trust in business was recorded (in answer to "I don't know which companies or brands to trust"[52]). The report for 2018 says that business is expected to lead on building trust. For CEOs, building trust is their prime responsibility. 64% of people say that CEOs should take the lead on change rather than waiting for government to impose it and that business must show long-term commitment to their stakeholders. The majority of respondents thought companies that only think about themselves and their profits are bound to fail and that CEOs are driven more by greed than a desire to make a positive difference in the world. The least trusted industry sector is the financial services, which is hardly surprising given the number of highly publicised corporate scandals in this sector over the last decade. This is where 21st century organisations can lead with instigating positive change which benefits a long reach of stakeholders rather than subverting legislation designed to protect the ultimate stakeholder, which is all of us (with reference to the Volkswagen emissions scandal here)!

The rise in initiatives that promote businesses as a force for good, benefiting people in their wider environment bears witness to the need to address the trust crisis. Two noteworthy examples are described in the following paragraphs.

B Lab is a non-profit enterprise that awards certification to organisations that seek to stand out from the industry norm as values-based and mission-driven. They want to show that they are socially and environmentally responsible, creating value for a broader set of stakeholders, not just their shareholders. The certification as a "B Corps" is awarded for "businesses that meet the highest standards of verified social and environmental performance, public transparency, and legal accountability to balance profit and purpose. B Corps are accelerating a global culture shift to redefine success in business and build a more inclusive and sustainable economy"[53]. There are currently more than 1,700 B Corporations in 50 countries[54].

Glassdoor, founded in 2007, has become a go-to resource for information that previously would have remained within company walls. It collects company reviews about workplaces, salaries, company culture etc. that are posted anonymously by existing and former employees, making what happens "on the inside" transparent for the general public. It publishes regular reports on the best and worst places to work and as such is considered a valuable source of crucial information for employers and jobseekers alike. It is now used by over 30 million members across the globe. Its founders noted the value of workplace transparency early on as well as the connection of brand to corporate culture:

A company's reputation is not built overnight nor is its employer brand, which must authentically and intrinsically tie into its mission and values. Smart companies recognize that a favourable employer brand not only influences candidates and enhances recruiting efforts, it also can influence your customers, partners, investors, and other stakeholders.

CEO of Glassdoor, Robert Hohman[55]

Building a trusting culture

Trust is a feature of a thriving 21st century company culture and given that it is a top priority for businesses to embrace, what is most needed to build it?

Building trust is a common theme in our work with individuals, teams and organisations. Where there is a lack of trust, performance suffers as people seek to protect their own interests from the untrusted other. Common complaints are rarely about the quality of products or services and mostly about interpersonal relationships although the "trust" issue is often raised in other ways. Trust seems to be a touchy subject; it seems too personal and painful to approach, something you shouldn't really talk about openly at work. If I don't trust my colleagues what does that say about me? By understanding the key issues that present when talking to individual team members we can get a sense of what themes will be most beneficial to address to raise trust levels and thus performance.

BUILDING TRUST IN TEAMS

Anne worked with the finance team of an international bank that had identified some "relationship and accountability issues" they felt were holding them back from achieving higher performance. To better understand this loose definition of the problem we used "the International Trust in Teams Indicator"[56], an online self-scoring assessment that measures nine different components of trust. In the debriefing session the team members worked together to discuss the results, agree on key findings and define specific actions they would take to improve. Subsequent meetings were held as progress checks and to further develop their understanding of the subject and more importantly each other. As a result of the team working together over time on the actions they had agreed, people outside the team reported a happier and more supportive team climate. Team results improved (e.g. measured by the delivery of more timely and dependable reports) and in turn enhanced the team's internal reputation as a solution provider (rather than an unwelcoming inspectorate).

Building trust externally, in your brand, has much to do with perseverance and consistency. It takes time and effort to make sure you are accessible to your clients, to know what value you can provide for them and deliver it. Transparency and honesty are needed as well as the courage to recognise and be open about what you can and cannot deliver to best meet the expectations of your stakeholders. Your solid reputation may have been built over decades but it can be lost in minutes in our global interconnected world. When values truly represent the behaviours in your organisation and stakeholders reap the benefits of the promises then your reputation will speak for itself, dismissing the need for "reputation management".

Examples of the ideal 21st century corporate culture

We have referred to the work of Frederic Laloux elsewhere and think his work relates to promises in many ways. Laloux's book *Reinventing Organisations*[57] has turned into a global phenomenon since it was first published in 2014 and has inspired countless organisations to adopt what Laloux calls "radically more soulful and purposeful"[58] management practices. We are convinced that it is possible to run organisations in ways that truly serve the people who work in them and the communities they impact. The many examples of those who have chosen the bold journey of "going teal" or at least adopting more purposeful practices prove the concept.[59]

Working with brand and culture

Dialogue with people in organisations is even more important when making the intangible (e.g. culture) visible because culture is the sum of what they live and experience.

When organisations recognise that they need some form of change initiative, a good place to start is with the values since if change does not proceed from the people, the chances for success are limited. Aligning with our GBL values of sustainability, holistic, integrity and partnership, we first bring the unconscious into awareness by working with people to discover their own stated and unstated values and what limits their full expression.

There is no one best way to develop culture, but a values-based, people-driven, emergent process gives a good foundation.

If a radical approach to a new kind of culture is not up for discussion in your organisation, there are many small steps that can all contribute to making a valuable, positive difference at work. Here is one example of an effective discussion teams can have, early in their engagement with each other. The aim is to help team members live up to their promises. The team makes time to discuss their expectations of each other and what they are prepared to offer in service of the team working at its potential. We call this "Offers" and "Wants". It's simple in its approach and can have a real impact on future relationships and thus team performance.

ACTIVITY

Offers and Wants

The following questions are asked of team members: In service of this team working at its full potential, what do we WANT from a) each other b) our leader c) us, as coaches.

What do we OFFER the team?

Discussion is first conducted in small groups (pairs if the team is small) and answers to the questions then pooled in order to come up with key themes. It's important in the facilitation to dig deeper than broad generalisations like "open and honest communication" and become really clear about what that looks, sounds and feels like (and what it isn't).

Having agreed and decided what everyone wants and offers, the next step is to draw up "team norms" or rules of conduct, whatever you want to call it. This should then be documented and revisited consistently, e.g. at the beginning of every team meeting. We find that team members are highly engaged in this activity, are pleased with their results and display commitment to putting the agreed norms into practice. Since change becomes embedded through ongoing focus, effort and repeated practice, it makes sense to end the session with a list of actions to support positive contributions and to flag up unhelpful behaviours. Consistent reminders by team members to each other reinforce the promises made and this has a ripple effect on others they interact with.

There are many ways of reinforcing and developing the kind of culture that you want to create. Our main point is that culture *is*, whether or not you take time to explore it. The implication is that ongoing conscious effort is required to shape the culture that serves your organisation that serves your stakeholders. We question the long-term viability of the big bang approach that dictates culture from the top of the organisation, involving huge outlays for a formal corporate programme roll-out and the support of armies of external consultants. We have experienced at first hand such programmes, been carried along by the excitement of the first wave and realised with regret over time that the huge efforts and resources invested did not reap the promised benefits. We are convinced on the other hand that culture change is possible if seeded and carried by positive influencers. This is a topic of great significance that goes beyond our remit here but we do want to mention the extraordinarily insightful approach pioneered by Dr Leandro Herrero, called "Viral Change"[TM60]. The five key ingredients in the Viral Change[TM] way of creating change according to Dr Herrero are:

- a small set of carefully chosen, specific, observable behaviours
- scalable influence (a relatively small number of individuals who have a high level of influence with their peers)
- informal networks
- stories to accelerate the new narrative (called "Weapons of Mass Diffusion")
- leaders who are highly trusted and well connected.

As an example, on the topic of safety in organisations, Herrero describes how a small set of "non-negotiable behaviours", once identified and spread across the organisation through "contagion", have the power to create a DNA of safety.[61]

PROMISES TO NEW EMPLOYEES

Here's a story of two new starters on the same day – an intern at a tech start-up and a new CEO for a medium-sized listed tech company, both in the City of London. We captured the reports of their first day and the promises that were made to them.

In the first story, the new CEO promises his staff at the internal company briefing "small" things that make a big difference like listening and asking questions and plenty of big things, like a new corporate culture and strategic direction. He has already worked out, by preparing in advance of his arrival, what the company needs, which is outlined in his strategic focus on building a customer-centric organisation with greater staff empowerment and pride. This comes with responsibility and he will hold people accountable. He envisages better customer relationships and higher growth. His tone is confident and his manner is one of optimism and high engagement. After all this final move in his long international career means that his lasting reputation is at stake.

In the second story, the student intern is delighted by his first day. The welcome was warm, the daily company breakfast "awesome", he reports of stories and stand-ups (nothing to do with comedy; this is agile language), of a lack of hierarchy, approachable, enthusiastic employees, and the sense that he is of value (since a company senior spent a whole hour of "line-and-box" meeting with him) and people invested their time in making him feel a part of the team from the start. Like every other employee, he is promised an hour of self-development investment time at the end of every day, to do what he likes. This he thinks shows commitment to independent thought and creativity as well as trusting people to make best use of this time. He has started his new job with a high degree of motivation and this is even before he knows what he will be doing there... that will transpire as specific project needs arise.

In both cases first impressions were very positive and only time will tell whether the promises made will be delivered upon so we followed up on both cases three months later. The first 100 days is often a marker for envisaged progress.

In the first story at the listed tech company, the reports are far from uplifting.

The stated approach of "collaboration" is lacking in its application. The CEO has plainly stated that it is his job to decide. Listening is not his style; he invites challenge but is not open to dialogue. His predominant style is commanding. As a result, senior company officials who were not considered compliant have been removed from the company. The CEO divides company employees into new (up to six months), medium tenure and the old guard (more than three years). He has made clear on a number of occasions in public that the old guard are responsible for all the company's problems. The new CEO's motto is "Everyone needs to be on the train. You are either part of the new way or you are out." People fear that the company does not have long-term viability and are exiting at all levels, including technical support specialists who have been on board for many years. Major transition issues are starting to emerge due to lack of knowledge transfer as headquarters expertise is lost to the company. Key to company success announced by the new CEO was to be a sharpened commercial focus, empowering salespeople to give of their best through mutual respect and accountability. Account directors have been given their budgets, without consultation. No negotiation was permitted and industry and regional boundaries have been redrawn (with the resulting loss of bonus potential for deals not yet signed but worked towards for the past years). A new sales manager joined the company and was introduced to the sales team without any advance warning. The incumbent key account director and sales director were not informed. The long-term relationship with the company's biggest client is at risk, and the client contact is upset that the replacement manager has no experience of their business and thinks he is incompetent.

In order to "get the brand right and create a winning culture", marketing consultants were hired to conduct an all-company "summer party" where the new company values were announced. Many initiatives are being conducted under the "new way" banner that could be powerful if they were accompanied by tangible demonstrations of real willingness to connect and reach the hearts as well as the minds of new and long-tenure company members. The missing ingredient seems to be a genuine caring for people that is the basis for building respect.

The second story is quite a different one. Here is the input written by the intern in response to how promises are being kept in his company.

"I like what you're saying in the promises chapter. We work on a massively complex system that no one here can say they completely understand. If we couldn't live up to our internal promises, in other words if the system would start to break, we would surely start losing customers. I've been told that the reason our product is used by many fortune 500 companies to deploy their code is because they trust that we have a mature and stable product. From what I've understood, the strategy is to be able to keep the product mature and stable, even if we have to switch out a massive part of our code base (something that will be happening in the next few years). They talk a lot about day 2. We don't just sell software and run it, we make sure that the software is working from day 2 and beyond."

In response to the question: to what extent do you feel that you have "lived the values" in your time at work so far, the intern said:

"'Living the values' – this certainly applies very well to my company. The main values are 'Do what works, do the right thing, be kind'. I feel like we do live these values. Do what works and do the right thing apply to how we work. Usually tech companies focus mostly on the first one, just getting things to work, but code here is more of a craft – it doesn't just have to work, it has to be done right. We've been working on a track of work for almost a month now, where they've been waiting to get this feature finished for a year I think, we've 'had a solution' for weeks, but it wasn't necessarily the right one, or well tested. Our solution didn't start to work in the entire system until we had been through several rounds of refactoring and testing solutions – this is what 'doing the right thing' is. Theoretically this solves a bunch of problems further down the line. I would agree to that.

"'Be kind' is how we treat each other. We spend most of our time working with each other, especially compared to other engineering companies – it can get quite intense. The reason I've felt welcome as an intern is because everyone spends a lot of effort just being nice to each other while working. It eases the tension that I think otherwise would quite easily arise."

The connection of culture and brand

The case described by the intern above shows that the internal promises allow the external promises to be fulfilled. This is what we mean by alignment or two sides of the same coin, a useful metaphor to summarise the connection between culture and brand. One side of the coin is the brand image: the way customers and society view the organisation from the outside. The other side is the culture: the way employees experience the organisation from the inside and communicate the brand values to the outside by their behaviour.

For the organisation to be authentic, both perspectives, culture and brand image, should demonstrate the same values. In other words, brand image should be reflected in your organisation's culture and your culture should be reflected in your brand image. When this does not happen people feel let down and take their services (employees) and their business (clients) elsewhere. Highly publicised examples are plenty (like Carillion in the UK) where organisations over-promise and under-deliver. When clients and investors lose trust these organisations crumble.

We can take charge of our promises and our stakeholder relationships by asking the promises questions and answering them truthfully (from the perspectives of multiple stakeholders). This helps us to measure consistency and take action to address any gaps.

QUESTIONS FOR REFLECTION

If you want to understand more about what is meant by "organisational culture", consider your answers to the following questions:

- **?** What do you love most about working here?
- **?** What do you have in common with the people who thrive at your company?
- **?** Which are the (unspoken) promises the company fulfils to you personally?

You may also think about the typical things you experience and don't like so much – if these are the same for a large number of people then they become blocks to performance that need addressing. (Typically in organisations these can include too much bureaucracy, poor leadership, blame culture, long working hours or unproductive working.)

- **?** What are the promises your team/organisation makes to your stakeholders?
- **?** Are the promises you make consistent to your different stakeholder groups?
- **?** Have you taken time to consider how your brand (the sum of our external promises) is perceived and how this matches what your customers and employees are experiencing at first hand?
- **?** What do you "promise" without being consciously aware that you are doing so?
- **?** How does your team/organisation serve its stakeholders?

? What is the image you portray to your stakeholders?

? How do you inspire your followers to serve your stakeholders?

? How do you deepen the connection with all your stakeholders?

? How do you co-create with your stakeholders?

? Where are the disconnects between promises and delivery?

CHAPTER SUMMARY

Here are the main points of Chapter 5:

> How internal promises (culture) and external promises (brand) are inter-related and that they need to be aligned for a 21st century organisation to survive and thrive

> How culture needs to adapt to change, which individual attitudes to change are needed and some activities to support change efforts

> How culture impacts brand experience through the sum of many individual experiences that create a lasting impression

> The role of trust in 21st century organisations

> Some pointers for building trust in teams

> Some examples of best practice

CHAPTER 6

Strategy

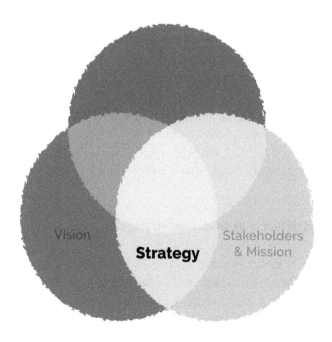

6. Strategy

Strategy is a word that's open to considerable interpretation – to us it means to design the right path to the best outcome. It can be at the whole enterprise level or a component of it.
John Caswell, Group Partners

Strategy lies at the intersection between stakeholders and mission and vision. The strategy questions aim to uncover **how** the team or organisation will deliver its mission, what plans are already in place and how these relate to stakeholder needs and vision. Strategy defines the steps needed to get from where we are now to where we want to be. It spells out how the value we are best positioned to create matches stakeholders' needs in a way that is aligned with values and purpose. From a Discovery Prism© perspective this value proposition should refer not just to what is to be done but *how* we should be. Strategy serves as a roadmap to deliver the mission and realise the vision, serving as a guide for people to successfully achieve the organisation's aims, doing the right things right. If it is well formulated it will be specific enough to test decisions and make judgments about priorities. As a cross check, if your stakeholders' expectations are not aligned with vision, you should consider what this strategy *will* deliver? Strategy is as much about what is left out as what is counted in.

Why is it important to be clear about strategy?

People need to understand how what they are doing and how they are "being" connects to the bigger picture. This gives a sense of purpose and direction. Everyone makes decisions and choices daily about what they do and how they work and, with few exceptions, people want to do a good job and contribute.

Even if the strategy decision-makers are clear about strategic focus amongst themselves, those needed to act it out, support the actors or who are recipients of the end product may still have very different expectations. Strategy is therefore an overlap lens representing a two-way exchange. It is informed from stakeholders and vision and in turn impacts both. The assumption too often with strategy is that everyone will automatically "get it" and execute accordingly. Unfortunately, research indicates that less than 5% of a typical employee group understands their organisation's strategy.[62]

This is where communication plays a critical role. It must be clear, consistent and make sense to different target groups. Key messages may need explaining and repeating many times for them to land.

> *The greatest problem with communication is the illusion that it has been accomplished.*
> George Bernard Shaw

Formulating the strategy

To be useful the strategy needs to evolve with changing circumstances yet be stable enough to provide guidance for key decision-making. It's a leader's job to keep balancing the fixed versus the flexible. Unless the leader is really connected to stakeholders' requirements, concerns, knowledge and insights, she will not have the input to achieve this balance. We operate in a world of unprecedented, disruptive change where whatever we have just agreed, produced or delivered may not be fit for purpose for very long. We are connected digitally to communities across the globe, opening up greater opportunities and also threats. The giants of industry have been taken unaware by competition from unsuspected quarters. Who was to have guessed a few years ago that the world's largest taxi company owns no taxis (Uber), the largest accommodation provider owns no real estate (Airbnb), that there are huge phone companies that own no telecoms infrastructure (Skype and WeChat). The largest movie house owns no cinemas (Netflix) and the most popular media owner creates no content (Facebook). Even financial institutions are being threatened from unexpected quarters. No banks would have considered Apple, Google or Alibaba as competitors a few years ago, but now they all do. You can probably think of examples in your own industry segment.

Our borders have been pushed back or dissolved. The term "glocalisation" refers to the combination of a global and local approach to business expansion into foreign markets and the need to adapt to local market conditions and customer preferences in order to compete with local rivals. Another hybrid term is "coopetition" to signify collaborating with competitors in order to best serve in the marketplace. The example of Microsoft and Intel is probably the best known (based on the recognition that Intel's chips become of increasing value in proportion to them running ever more powerful Microsoft software). The fluid versus fixed dilemma permeates organisations on all levels. It's also the name of the game for people in their daily workplaces. Work teams are increasingly remote and virtual. Some project teams have rotating membership. Many work more virtually than locally without realising it and adjust behaviour accordingly. (Virtual is defined as anything that uses a medium other than person-to-person in the same physical space.[63]) Modern workplaces are not fixed either, providing hot-desking or activity-based environments as a concept that is more suited to differing requirements.

In the connected age, one person can no longer be expected to know all the answers, the one on whom all rely. As many eyes and ears as possible are needed to understand the business context and know how best to satisfy key stakeholders while playing to our strengths.

PwC summarised a key finding from their Global CEO Survey (2015): "More than anything, though, they'll [CEO's] have to develop a flexible vision that allows them to pinpoint their company's strengths even as their customers, sectors and markets change in front of their eyes."[64]

A further reason for the lack of clear strategy formulation is the confusion around terminology. It's not always easy to decide when strategic becomes "operational" and how much detail is needed. A senior leadership team called us in to help them find clarity after they had already had a strategy planning away day. A prior session had resulted in an unwieldy document that even the participants found difficult to read and act upon. In fact it wasn't referenced at all in subsequent work. The initial strategy session had been useful in that it had provided the opportunity for the directors to air their thoughts and ideas but they had gone overboard in the formulation of their strategic aims. Strategy had spilled over into operational plans and they realised that in order for the strategy to be useful and for it to be communicated with the right intent they needed to clarify and simplify. This became the primary aim of the second strategy session so that all directors could agree and pull in the same direction.

People don't always speak up when confused or dissatisfied with the end results. This stops real connection and is an example of a "trust leak". Valuable insights are withheld that could contribute to a richer discussion, even if they cause conflict. This happens typically where there is a lack of trust and the limiting fear of not being smart/strategic/visionary enough. It takes a lot of courage to raise awareness of the "elephant in the room"; fear and egos get in the way. For the most effective team cultures, these are the behaviours which need to change to build trust in the team. Trust is the key ingredient towards successful outcomes.

A way of checking the scope of strategy and necessary level of detail is to start with a clear definition of what strategy is and why it's important, agree the desired outcomes and keep referring to these. Questions to ask are "When will we know that this is formulated well enough to proceed?", "What next steps follow on from this (that we need to cover now, or later)?", "What is our definition of the line between strategy and operations?" and "What will be our knock-out questions for deciding what's in and what's out?" Strategy is about doing "the right things right" because anything else would be a complete waste of valuable resources.

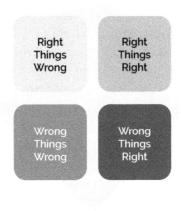

Figure 16 **Right vs Wrong Things Grid**

At the beginning of the strategy discussion, agree a way for any participant to raise the flag when the topic is going off track from the defined limits, particularly where people start diving into tactics. Linking back to the vision helps – tactics deliver the strategy, the strategy delivers the vision. Strategy answers how, where to, when by; the business plan is how much, who by where, with measurable milestones/metrics/targets.

Although everything around us may be changing and we feel increasingly unsettled by the lack of predictability, the one constant is the nature of human relationships and the importance of building trust. The nature or location of our business makes no difference; what matters more than anything else is that partners, inside and outside the business, believe we are "trustworthy". For strategy formulation it means understanding how trust can be best built in your markets (acknowledging that separate national and organisational cultures around the world have differing preferences for doing so). Even in cultures that are more "task" than relationship-oriented, where the focus is on short-term gains, trust is not built overnight, but in the constancy of approach and the keeping of commitments.

Strategy approaches old style, new style

Traditionally, organisations have defined their progress and success in terms of financial results alone (e.g. revenue, profit, return on investment, shareholder value). As a result, the strategy is honed to financial targets. As discussed already, it is no longer sufficient to focus solely on the bottom line (if it ever was!). Companies are increasingly measured (internally as well as externally) by their ability to contribute. They are rated not just in terms of what they have achieved in the past but on what they are currently undertaking in their various stakeholder communities both near and far and what they plan to leave as a legacy for future generations.

> *Profit is like the air we breathe. We need air to live, but we don't live to breathe.*
> Frederic Laloux[65]

Strategy planning starts with deciding who is responsible for formulating the strategy and implementing it. It's generally the role of the leader(s) to decide but not always to implement and depends on the size of the organisation. In smaller organisations the roles may fall to the same person or team. In large organisations the traditional way is to form a dedicated "Corporate Strategy Planning" unit that uses processes and strategic planning systems, often with high costs in terms of staff and time committed to analysis and testing. Many of the most elaborate strategies never get implemented or only in part. When this happens, the connections are often missing – strategy formulation and implementation are seen as separate entities and when the strategy is finally unveiled it may fail to reap the admiration of those who have not been involved, but are expected to deliver to the plans. There is a link between involvement in the process and being motivated to take action.

Buy-in to ideas is more likely to take place when there has been an involvement of some sort at discussion level even when the final decision is made by someone else. Where strategy is not implemented well or even at all, it is often the case that the strategy planning team has failed to inform and gather input from those who would be most affected by subsequent changes. The planners commonly feel the need to "prove their worth" by spelling everything out to the final detail and thus reduce the engagement of the implementers and any accountability too. When things don't work out as planned, the implementers are quick to blame the planners rather than look at mutual opportunities to come up with creative solutions to navigate the hurdles. We have tested this hypothesis using an activity called "The Production Unit"[66] for international leaders attending a leadership development programme. Although the key themes of "collaboration" and "inclusive leadership" were known to all participants, we observed that only in a small minority of cases did planners and implementers decide to pool their ideas and talents at an early stage. Those who did consistently achieved the best results to the frustration of their divided colleagues. In other words a strategy of collaboration won over one of competition!

New approaches to strategy: collaborative, emergent, holistic

Strategy has been determined for generations from a problem-solving point of view, regarding the competition as the entity to beat to gain bigger rewards, a larger share of the market etc. and has been implemented in a linear fashion. We are not saying that our planet has unlimited resources but we do question the notion of a "limited pie" and argue for a mindset of abundance rather than one of scarcity in how we meet each other and our marketplace. Given the VUCA circumstances, as far as strategy is concerned we need to apply new more emergent approaches since predictions that result from past performance seem to bear increasingly little relevance to what could happen and what actually does! In addition, as generally agreed today, a wider perspective needs to be taken, recognising and connecting all parts as elements of the whole.

One such approach taken by managers who successfully implement their strategy demonstrates the benefits of trial and error over time. In the past this has been called "logical incrementalism"[67], describing a process where managers implement smaller steps and improve the quality of information on which key decisions are based. Ongoing work aims to raise awareness and overcome expected resistance to change from internal and external players, demonstrating an understanding for what motivates people to support (or block). Processes are developed to reflect learning from customer insights and to take account of the organisational culture. This approach means that strategies are developed incrementally so that some parts are being implemented as other parts are not yet fully defined. The aim is to build sufficient momentum within the organisation to carry forward the planned changes in a more flexible, ongoing way. Logical incremental approaches have been in use for more than half a century although the term is attributed to Quinn to explain how companies devise their strategies in the real world.

The agile methodology in software development is a more modern term that has its roots in logical, incremental approaches. Agile has spread beyond the boundaries of software companies as a strategy that welcomes change. The methods are adaptive, incremental and iterative as well as being people oriented. They also allow a high degree of creativity. The aim is to support development teams in determining the best way to fulfil the task in hand in accordance with defined and emerging needs and in collaboration with the customer.

These more agile, emergent approaches mean that strategy can be adjusted to take account of today's shifting and volatile environment. Though the "line of sight" from a person's work to the big picture can become clouded, ongoing communication channels will be in place to keep clarifying strategic shifts. Such approaches are as much about the "being" as the "doing" and thus how strategy comes into being is of the essence. Transparent communication is conducted consciously from the outset.

Communicating the strategy: the role of role models

Communication of the strategy is a sub-strategy itself! In other words, consideration needs to be given to how messages land from different stakeholder perspectives, what is to be delivered, how frequently, to whom and by which means. Of course this is much easier if the strategy has emerged from engagement with stakeholders. They will provide the language to express what they do and don't want. If an integrated approach to strategy formulation has been taken, communication will already be at its most effective, using all senses during the process, values and purpose-led. In other words, "communication" is not just an add-on element when all else has been completed and is to be considered consciously from the outset. As Cisco executives Ron Ricci and Carl Wiese say:

When everyone speaks the same language, it's a lot easier to keep collaborative teams on track to achieve results. Establishing a common vocabulary for how you communicate decisions and identify the people accountable for the outcomes of those decisions will minimize second guessing and confusion so teams can move faster.[69]

Communication must be considered in all its forms – not just printed matter, digital presence, but particularly about how all messages are delivered, verbally and non-verbally, by whom, in which context and with which intention. How do you seed the right messages? To stay true to your values and vision, keep asking "are we putting our attention on our intention?" What are the outcomes you are looking for and are you taking into account the particular situation of your different stakeholder groups? Are you displaying accountability? For example, when you announce a new strategy, indeed any kind of change, those who are affected either directly or indirectly will naturally seek reassurance. This is particularly the case where strategy is dictated from the top without prior involvement or collaboration. Excitement at the top tier is not necessarily mirrored across the organisation. Big changes may create a huge sense of uncertainty (What do I risk losing? Will I still be needed? Will I have a job? etc.). When people know that change is afoot, the rumours fly, so it makes sense to communicate as much as possible as early as possible in the process. This includes what is not being discussed or has been considered and discarded because of the speed at which news travels, bad news particularly fast. In an era where fake news is also considered news the need for truth is more in demand than ever before.

The formal or informal leaders in any group have the greatest impact on emotional climate; as such they should be particularly conscious of how accurately their words and deeds mirror intention at whatever stage in the process. A leader delivered his collaboration strategy as the new way for the company to move forward but used the "I" word so many times that the message did not appear to be authentic. It can be useful to listen for the use of "I" or "we" language to understand how inclusive the speaker (or writer) is at heart. If the formal leaders of the organisation do not role model the intent in the best way, someone else will!

Strategy is best delivered by those with a high degree of influence and communicated with positive intent, so that messages are not undermined or lost in translation.

> *The simple man can become the most powerful and the most influential because he is connected and grounded.*
> Joan Planes, Fluidra

Strategy mapping

The strategy can be recorded visually from the outset – this is what is known as strategy mapping. Since the ensuing map is agreed by all participants it becomes a key document for communication. The map itself can take many forms and can become the focal point for ongoing discussion, showing connections, giving direction and supporting decision-making. By omission, it indicates what is **not** a priority.

At the recent Map Camp conference in London, speaker Janet Hughes spoke from her experience of managing and supporting major projects. She is Director, Major Projects and Head of Project Delivery Profession at the Department of Education for the UK government. Janet currently oversees 39 major projects.

"What we need is to make sense of complexity, to speak a common language, to prioritise all things and to find a way to make shared decisions. Therefore, we need to map!"

Wardley Mapping[70] is a collaborative activity that starts with examining the landscape, or the wider system context. An example is shown in Figure 17. Having understood what key stakeholders need, the mapping process offers a way to map the relationship between all the components that support the need. The next step is to understand how mature (or evolved) these components are and whether they are changing. The advantage of this methodology is that it helps to pinpoint critical elements (that were perhaps obvious in hindsight but not at the time). The step-by-step approach allows users to identify what is visible and hidden, what are differentiation factors and which elements have separate needs. By having more clarity about elements that are critical and of high value, priorities can be allocated and decisions made about what needs delivering, when and how. Users report huge savings in time and money from the mapping process which visualises the complexity of projects and often highlights areas of duplication, misalignment, pain points and missed connections.[71]

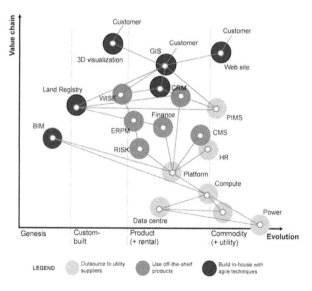

Figure 17 **Example of a Wardley Map**
(courtesy of Leading Edge Forum)

Ken Wilber's Integral Map[72] or operating system is an example of a completely different kind of map reflecting a trend in increasingly popular holistic approaches. Such multiple-disciplinary approaches combine learning and research from the sciences, spiritual and philosophical teachings as well as ancient wisdom. The study of energy, quantum physics and neuroscience as well as the ancient philosophers are becoming more commonplace today in business literature with regard to leadership development and organisational life.

Where to start with strategy?

When coaching individuals and teams we often refer to Marshall Goldsmith's Change Wheel. This is useful to clarify what is positive or detrimental in our current situation, what we want to change and what we want to keep or may need to accept. It is a very simple, yet highly practical starting place to start creating a new strategy or to revisit an existing one. A highly performing team had plenty to preserve, acknowledging what was working for them. As they reflected together they also became aware that an essential ingredient of their success was how they supported each other to best lead their own teams as well as being powerful members of their own top team. They decided that their strategy needed a greater focus on "being" in order to balance the "doing" and this became a useful indicator for their progress towards achieving their defined purpose.

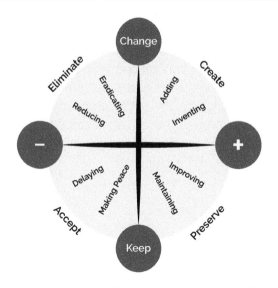

Figure 18 **The Wheel of Change (used with permission of Marshall Goldsmith)**

So how do you honour what has gone before while embracing new approaches that will still deliver "success" however this is defined? There are a number of effective approaches, the choice of which should depend on any number of factors like the size of the organisation, its current appetite for change and how compelling the push and pull factors are. The following examples are provided as alternatives to traditional strategy planning and implementation. Their various approaches can be described as emergent, collaborative and holistic, which enable 21st century organisations to thrive.

Values-based strategies

One example of a values-based approach to strategy definition is relevant if you have already chosen to map your values using the Barrett Values Cultural Transformation Tools© (as described in Chapter 3). The result of the Cultural Values Assessment© (CVA) provides a good starting point for defining a balanced business strategy in the form of the Business Needs Scorecard© (BNS).[73] This outlines where the business is focusing its energies currently (the values of the current culture) and where employees would like to see future change (the desired culture). Research shows that organisations that focus on employee needs (such as those in Best Companies to Work for[74] and care for all their stakeholders (so-called Firms of Endearment) are considerably more successful and resilient than other organisations.[75]

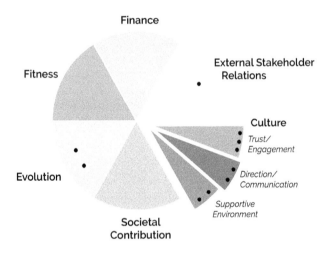

Figure 19 **Example of a Business Needs Scorecard (© Barrett Values Centre)[76]**

Here's an example of a group corporate strategy using the house pillars diagram. The values provide the foundation and underpin the whole approach.

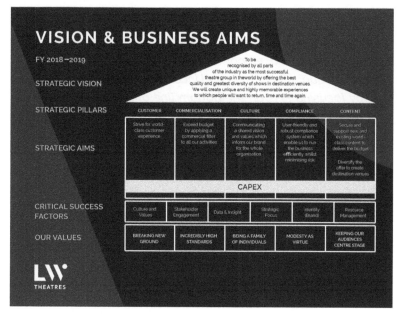

Figure 20 **Strategy Map from LW Theatres**

Teal organisations

As mentioned in the Stakeholders and Mission chapter, Frederic Laloux calls the future of management "teal". In his book *Reinventing Organizations*, Laloux argues the case for a new kind of management to lead and inspire the organisations of the future, since the traditional way of running and structuring organisations is limiting potential in today's VUCA world. He refers to best practice examples of organisations that have been highly successful and profitable over the long term. The common denominator is that all adopted self-management practices; they are "soulful" organisations where people have a deep sense of purpose and demonstrate "wholeness". People feel fully free to express who they are, not just from a limited view of what is professional and acceptable; they bring their whole selves to work. This is how Laloux how describes "evolutionary purpose"[77]:

> *Teal organizations base their strategies on what they sense the world is asking from them. Agile practices that sense and respond replace the machinery of plans, budgets, targets and incentives. Paradoxically, by focusing less on the bottom line and shareholder value, they generate financial results that outpace those of competitors.*

The change strategy Laloux proposes is incremental, driven by the greatest perceived need and tested on a smaller scale. The organisations surveyed did not announce big culture changes but evolved through undertaking small, low cost, low risk experiments with ongoing learning and tweaks to the processes being implemented (i.e. a prototyping approach). He suggests that the starting point is to understand the current energy blocks, asking where people feel the pain. Different organisations raise different things. For some it may be the "smoke and mirrors" type of budgetary process game that people play in spite of predicted numbers being unrealistic and becoming quickly outdated. For others it may be the performance measurement process that doesn't honour the desired values of the company and creates distrust through rewarding the wrong behaviours.

An integrated approach to strategy planning

An example of an integrated approach to strategy planning is Alan Seale's **Manifestation Wheel**[78]. What we particularly like about using this is that it includes all facets of the Discovery Prism© in its cycle of aligning energies to bring a desired outcome.

The Manifestation Wheel is developed from the study of ancient teaching wisdom traditions as well as the principles of quantum physics. Seale's foundation is the ancient Lakota Medicine Wheel which he has updated in terms of language and concepts in order to make it applicable to today's world. The Medicine Wheel is a central tenet of North American Indian philosophy and as interpreted by the Lakota tribe draws on their principles of egalitarianism, participation and reciprocity – age-old concepts that are undergoing revival in organisations and societies today.

> *In sum, the Medicine Wheel brings together the teachings of the circle, such as egalitarianism, reciprocity, natural democracy, complementarity, and a participatory view of the relationship between humanity and nature, with the central importance of balance as an ideal in Lakota philosophy.*[79]

The Medicine Wheel describes a process we might now call project management and was used to guide the Lakota in making decisions, getting things done, managing relationships and conflicts. Alan Seale has brought the language and concepts up to date for today's world. You might want to use it yourself – it's a powerful tool for bringing your visions and dreams to life. We put our book project on it – you are reading the outcome!

What is a successful strategy – how will you know?

Common to all of the practices referred to above is that for a strategy to be effective, it has to be grounded (emerge from what is), and find the balance between flexible and fixed as well as fit for purpose, honouring the people it will impact. There is hope for more "soulful" or whole-hearted organisations and many smaller scale practices that can be applied locally over time will impact the greater entity. Incremental, emergent approaches make it possible for people to tap into their greatest creative potential to make a lasting positive difference, if they are encouraged to participate in an active way. Change doesn't happen overnight but rather in the practice of many small steps in the chosen direction, where commitment and limitless belief in the potential of the collective are key ingredients.

Strategy defines the action to deliver the vision. Imperfect action is better than no action at all. People limit themselves by believing the strategy or resulting plan needs to be "perfect" or fully developed before getting to the action. Ask yourself if the choice is "good enough" for now, or "safe enough" to give it a go. Perfection (even if it exists) can be a paralysing concept and completion a misnomer, because who is to say when something is "good enough", "ready enough", "finished enough"? Most things are, as human beings, a work in progress.

The best evidence of a successful strategy is the renewed energy it releases.

QUESTIONS FOR REFLECTION

? What are your current main strategic priorities?

? What are the challenges in defining them?

? How much detail do you need?

? What assumptions are you making?

? What limits and holds you back (including beliefs, attitudes of self and others)?

? How does your strategy enable you to deliver on your promises to your stakeholders?

? What differentiates you and how can you make the most of your differentiation?

? How does your strategy link to your vision and purpose?

? To what extent does it reflect your corporate values?

? How do you communicate what is important and to whom?

? How clearly is your strategy communicated?

? How much do people buy in to your strategy (leaders, team members and externally)?

? What resources and assets do you need to deliver your strategy?

? How targeted and focused is it?

? Is it sustainable for the required length of time?

? How often will it be revisited and by whom?

? Is it actionable?

? How will you deliver your plan? What will get in the way?

? How can you gather insights and learning in an ongoing way and incorporate them into your strategy?

? What new processes will you need to deliver your strategy?

? What no longer serves you? What current processes will need updating or removing?

? How will you become aware of your changing environment and stakeholder needs?

? How will you measure results and correct your course as the context around you shifts?

? What is the potential waiting to happen?

? What are your measures of success?

CHAPTER SUMMARY

Here are the main points of Chapter 6:

> Understanding how strategy connects to vision, stakeholder and mission

> How the communication of strategy is critical to its successful implementation

> That strategy doesn't need to be complex in its definition and implementation to be successful

> Some useful pointers for keeping strategy formulation on track

> That there is a balance to be struck between fixed and flexible and that one person (the leader) can't do it all alone

> Why new approaches to strategy (that are collaborative, emergent and holistic) are most suited to managing and thriving in the 21st century

> Some examples of new approaches and how to tell they are successful

CHAPTER 7

Legacy

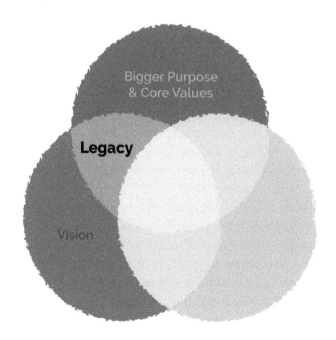

7. Legacy

Perhaps the ultimate test of a leader is not what you are able to do in the here and now - but instead what continues to grow long after you are gone.
Tom Rath[80]

What is legacy?

The overlap of the bigger purpose, core values and vision lenses creates the legacy overlap lens. The core purpose and values (Chapter 2) provide the **why** we are here and the **how** we act whilst vision (Chapter 3) brings the **where** we are going and **when** we will get there. Legacy stimulates thinking about how the vision will impact future generations and whether our bigger purpose can be discerned in the resulting trail. Reflecting on legacy can be useful in the present both to test the impact of past strategy on stakeholders as well as to guide future actions and behaviour. When you think deeply about legacy there are various time dimensions in play: you are assessing how your vision of the future will impact the past to inform how and what you work on in the present. What is the legacy you are leaving for each of your stakeholders? Are you leaving the legacy that aligns with your vision and purpose? What are the elements providing the evidence of your legacy? What will history judge you for and does that make you proud? The legacy you leave **is** the realised vision. It connects and creates the balance between achievement and endowment. To consider legacy is to bring into the present future generations as a key stakeholder. How to consciously create your legacy is the rationale behind this chapter.

Why is legacy important?

Are you concerned about what you leave behind for future generations? If your answer is "no" then read no further. And if your answer is "yes", then the question becomes all about what that is and how you go about it.

The growth of the internet and social media has brought a corresponding growth of companies specialising in reputation management, a concept which originated in public relations agencies. Why reputation management is deemed so important today is because bad news about an organisation (whether true or not) spreads fast and can have such an adverse impact on reputation. This computes to a corresponding loss in stock value. Companies ranked reputation as their top risk in 2017 according to Aon (the insurance broker).[81] The recent case of Nike reinstating the controversial footballer Colin Kaepernick as an image-bearer of the brand underlines this. (The initial unveiling of the ad attracted more than 80 million views on social media.)[82]

Legacy as it is conceived in the Discovery Prism© has nothing to do with spin, or with adjusting perception of behaviour to justify or redeem reputation. It is about consciously behaving in alignment with vision, purpose and values – it is both a concept to raise awareness, to awaken us to what is important, and manifestation – the gift of our endeavours to those who remain long after our departure.

Good or bad legacy?

Unconscious legacies can be both negative or positive. Do people smile when you come into a room or when you leave it? The legacy you leave has a direct correlation with how others trust you and interact with you. Unless they are consciously purged, the result of past leaders' negative legacies are felt energetically in organisations long after those leaders have moved on. One specific leader's legacy was the reticence of senior managers to speak up. When challenged by the new MD who was used to more interaction and challenge from his senior team, the latter lamented that this had been previously discouraged. Like birds who have only known cages all their life, they had to be coaxed to fly again.

Another HR professional bemoaned the existence of "legacy coaches" in her organisation, coaches the organisation had employed for so long that they were no longer able to reflect the patterns that were holding back the company. Instead of being part of the solution these legacy coaches had become part of the system. Yet another leader shared how the organisation regretted underestimating the impact of their presence in the local community. It had been their intention to give back by supporting local schools. In effect, they became such an attractor for incoming talent that property prices became inflated and locals were driven out.

In considering legacy you do therefore have to consider the existing internal legacies which may be impacting individuals/ teams/the organisation to their detriment as well as the desired legacy which will benefit future generations internally and externally. In common with the other lenses, the legacy that is co-created is consciously chosen and collectively endorsed. When this happens it results in an organisation that is both self-aware and aware of its stakeholders, taking responsibility for what it creates.

Experience and knowledge of the past can often be enemies of the creativity required to take forward steps. The slump into "we tried stuff before and it didn't work" or "that could never work here" can be declared as the final judgement on the failure of initiatives so that staying stuck in the unsatisfactory present seems the only option. Questioning how something didn't work and what *could* work is itself an act of creativity. Working with limiting legacies to identify them as "what holds us back" can ensure they become the foundational spur to innovation and progress.

The simple grid that follows breaks down how legacy can affect an organisation. In 21st century organisational terms the distinction between internal and external is a fluid one as Chapter 5 on promises shows. What affects the team internally will eventually leak externally. In saying this, however, the model may prove useful in narrowing those areas in which elements of legacy can be traced, so any negative inheritance can be dealt with before effects become endemic.

LEGACY	INTERNAL	EXTERNAL
UNDESIRABLE	Limiting Potential	Damaging & Limited Brand
DESIRABLE	Maximising Potential	Alignment & Congruence Enhancing Brand

Figure 21 **Tracing Legacy Grid**

Questions to help uncover the legacies in each quadrant can be thought of from an individual/team or organisational perspective:

Internal

1. What/who have been the significant influences on you/ the team/the organisation (it could be former bosses, a particular project, change initiative, shuffle, merger etc)? Don't limit it by timescale. People refer to long-departed CEOs. (A client once went as far back as "the war" but this is probably a unique case.)

2. What are the effects that persist as a result? They could be both positive and/or negative: lack of trust, a sense of collective responsibility, side conversations, silo working, ability to admit mistakes.

3. How do these show up and what do they limit/enhance? Think of who you hire, how they are inducted, how much capacity is given for people to be creative, behaviours in meetings, how you deal with mistakes, how you incorporate learning.

4. What do you want to keep/adapt/change?

5. What will success look like?

6. Thank those significant influences for the learning they have imparted and remove them with the recognition that they no longer serve the system.

External

1. What is your impact on stakeholders?

2. What is the "received history" of the relationship with key stakeholders? What stories are passed on to newer contacts potentially affecting future relations?

3. What do you need to test the reality of that impact? (The evidence will depend on the nature of the stakeholder – it may be staff retention, feedback, external metrics, quality of relationships.)

4. What will future generations thank you for?

5. How far does this impact align with your vision?

6. How far does this impact fulfil your sense of Purpose?

7. What do you need to become more conscious of?

8. What adjustments are needed and how do you implement them?

What is your legacy?

The most common time we hear the term legacy is at someone's death. The will is a legal document listing any physical assets. The less physical but albeit tangible legacy however is the impact or reputation which remains of the person after their departure. How are they remembered? What was the lasting impression made on family, friends, colleagues and strangers? A highly respected CEO remained within the company he had led, taking a secondary role to the new CEO. The former CEO undermined the new one at every turn and it was only when a coach helped him realise he was damaging his own previously high reputation in the organisation that he revised his behaviour. More than money and status, his reputation was the most important thing and the last thing he wanted to compromise.

ACTIVITY

The Rocking Chair exercise (or sometimes called "funeral eulogy") is a common method used in coaching to get people to connect with their vision, core values, purpose and legacy. They are asked to imagine themselves at a ripe old age rocking comfortably on a chair (or listening to their eulogies from a floating vantage point at a remembrance service) to survey and assess their lives. As they look back what are they most proud of? What has been manifest in their lives? What is the impact they have made? What is most important to them? What will they be remembered for? Once these questions are fully explored the most important question of all, once back in the present day in the full capacity of the present, is what's the next step to make those milestones happen? Is there anything they need to change now to realise what they want to be remembered for? Could there be unintended consequences that subvert the legacy they want to leave?

We have to act to create a conscious legacy. It is not a passive activity.

The Time Line is a similarly powerful exercise. Members of a team are asked to line up from left to right according to the duration of belonging to the team from the shortest time to the longest. The individuals in the team talk from their position of longevity. The older hands can acknowledge the legacy that came before them and how things have changed. There is an acknowledgement of their contribution to the team's current position. The newest members often have a fresh perspective and can relay what has become invisible to others. Everyone, from their unique position on the timeline, brings an insight – and, in acknowledging the different legacies, the possibility of a new team legacy emerges.

Amongst the many rich nuggets to emerge from this exercise is an expansion of presence of participants. It seems that by soliciting from people what they uniquely offer from their time perspective, something important has been unblocked, allowing a kind of settling which acts as a springboard to the future. In Discovery Prism© terms their own specific lens has been explored and brought into consciousness. Individual contributions are now at the disposal of the collective, expanding everyone's view and shedding light on what may have been poorly understood in the past.

As referenced in the Tracing Legacy Grid (Figure 21), reflecting on legacy may be instrumental in removing unconscious blocks that cause a disconnect with vision. When there is conscious alignment of the internal (core purpose, values, vision for the organisation) and the external (legacy and all stakeholders), the unconscious does not have to offer up resistance as there is nothing left to protect. By contrast providing the opportunity for people across an organisation to reflect on and express their ideas about legacy and how that aligns with the other lenses of the Discovery Prism© enables connection and a resultant boost of engagement with the organisation's goals. This is the key to all these conversations and focus on the lenses: the identification of the individual with the organisation without surrendering their uniqueness – a harnessing not an engulfing – not *its* goals but **our** goals, not *its* aspirations but **our** aspirations, **our** legacy.

For some, commitment to legacy is about giving back. The story of a local small business exemplifies this. Helen knew about the tangible legacies this business had left in the community and wanted to demonstrate how the size of a business is no barrier to making a huge impact. The only obstacle was that she knew that this business had recently closed its doors, five years after being inaugurated in 2012. When the business closed, there was an outpouring of support on social media and local people alluded to the closure as a personal loss. Such was the impact of the business, in both the tangible and intangible legacies, that she wanted to speak to the founder and hear his story first hand.

ABSOLUTE RUNNING

Nick Carter and his son **Harry** set up **Absolute Running** selling sports equipment to make running more accessible to people in Gosport, Hampshire and to involve people in sporting activities. Their wider purpose was about health and well-being as running was not the only activity they boosted amongst the local community. According to national statistics, Gosport was fifth on the list of the most obese towns and their vision was to turn this around. To get the business off the ground, Nick and his son first tried mainstream advertising which was expensive offering little return. Engagement, however, was immediate when they turned their attention to social media. The platforms gave them visibility but it was their willingness to respond and interact authentically with the community that effectively launched the business.

As part of giving back to the local community Nick and Harry announced they would put a safety boat in the sea on Friday evenings for anyone who wanted to swim. Sixty people turned up on the first day and it became a regular weekly fixture. Nick thought a triathlon for Gosport was the next logical step and a committee was formed that has taken on a life of its own, encouraging all levels of expertise to compete. Nick and Harry also established the Golden Mile/5k races including wheelchair events. Nick proudly states that the Golden Mile start and finish lines, etched along the promenade of Stokes Bay, are visible on Strava[83]. It is a visible legacy.

The values of giving back were also evident in their customer service. If you were purchasing running shoes, they would take the time to analyse your gait and if within a month you experienced any problems, you could return them.

So much for ticking all the lenses of the Discovery Prism© – purpose, core values, promises, vision, mission, stakeholders and legacy. Alignment and congruence are evident in how they all connect. So what went wrong? Many a small business owner will relate to taking too much on and not delegating enough and with the benefit of hindsight Nick sees where help should have been sought before he became overwhelmed. However, this is not the end of the story.

Because of the residual support and goodwill from the community for Absolute Running, a larger company has now bought the business and Nick will be retained to manage it. This intangible goodwill (intangible in terms of the balance sheet) attracted their commercial interest. Nick is excited to be able to continue to do what he enjoys doing most which is serving his customers and his community. On learning of the business reopening a previous customer burst into tears of joy. In terms of the framework, the interconnection of all the lenses has created resilience at the Prism source. What was perhaps not present at an individual level has emerged in the collective, this whole being bigger than the sum of its parts. The company has survived initial closure because the connection to the community and its legacy is so palpable. People sense and experience the congruence between the internal and external messages and activity of the business.

The example of Absolute Running shows how the legacy of low cost sporting activities links directly to bigger purpose – to increase the health and well-being of the local population, and their vision of making sporting more accessible to the community (including the wheelchair bound). There are mutually reinforcing legacies for different stakeholder groups: the legacy of unparalleled service for the customer of sporting gear from the shop and the legacy of sporting fixtures accessible to all for the wider community. At national level the hope is, over time, that this will reduce the town's rankings in the obesity tables.

A further aspect of legacy which is highlighted reflecting on Nick and Harry's story is the concept of pride. Pride not as ego but as joy, pleasure and satisfaction in living your values so concretely.

The opposite of leaving a legacy, something you are proud of for future generations, means not only that you don't leave anything of value, but you leave future generations to sort out the mess left behind. When we don't think of legacy up front, it reduces the potential of the present and becomes a cost for the future.

In our interconnected world we cannot afford to ignore legacy as part of what is offered to all of our stakeholders. If businesses of any size are to thrive in the 21st century, the connection of all the lenses helps build resilience. Legacy judges the consistency between vision, purpose, values, promises, mission and stakeholders and earns the trust of future generations by including them as a present stakeholder. Reflecting on legacy will pay real dividends for the organisation internally and externally, helping both to avoid pitfalls and to make the vision more concrete.

QUESTIONS FOR REFLECTION

? What legacy do you want to leave?

? How would you like to be talked about and remembered?

? What are the unwanted/positive legacies impacting you currently?

? What is your current impact on your stakeholders?

? What would you like it to be?

? What's important to you about your legacy?

? What drives you and your team towards building your legacy?

? How do you make your team's desired legacy real to all your stakeholders?

? How important is your reputation now, and in the future?

CHAPTER SUMMARY

Here are the main points of Chapter 7:

> How legacy relates to other lenses in the Discovery Prism©

> The relationship of legacy to time: future, present and past

> The difference between reputation management
and legacy

> Unconscious negative legacy versus conscious
positive legacy

> Internal and external legacy

> How considering legacy harnesses potential by unblocking
resistance

> The link between sustainability and legacy

CHAPTER 8

The Prism

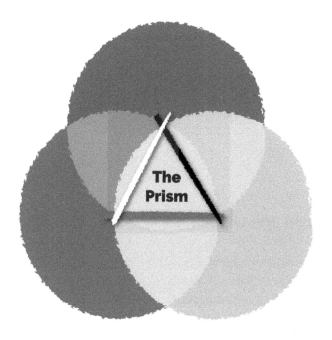

8. The Prism

When the individual and organizational purpose enter into resonance and reinforce each other extraordinary things can happen.
Frederic Laloux[84]

We have come to the final element of the Discovery Prism© which sits in the middle, at the epicentre of all the other lenses, and which is the Prism referred to in the framework title. It's the emergent whole-system space which has been discovered by exploring the other lenses. Our premise is that when you have worked collectively to bring each lens into closer focus you can sense and understand things with fresh perspectives. This work enables a shift – a different way of seeing with greater clarity. In terms of the metaphor of the prism, the individual colours of the lenses combine in the middle to create an intense white light which represents a communal energy in which the individual is still present. This energy re-energises each of the lenses in turn with the insights and coherence distilled at its core. The white light is greater than the sum of all its parts and in turn reflects back something more powerful to all those who have contributed. It can be experienced as a palpable positive energy, opening up unforeseen possibilities.

The Prism and wholeness

The link between wholeness and the Prism can perhaps be better understood by looking at the link between wholeness and an individual. In his book *On Becoming a Leader*, Warren Bennis says "the process of becoming a leader is similar, if not identical, to becoming a fully integrated human being".[85]

The nature of a *fully integrated human being* could be debated indefinitely. Perhaps it doesn't stretch Bennis' words to suggest it includes the idea of someone seamless or whole, someone who walks their talk, who is grounded, who most would agree operates close to their full human potential. The elements of wholeness could include congruence of thought, word and action. Someone who remains true to themselves no matter the audience. Someone of integrity (another word for wholeness) who inspires trust and has a sense of abundance rather than scarcity. Someone grounded, and effective. This would be a powerful and influential individual whatever his or her assigned hierarchical role. This individual has nothing to defend and can explore with an open perspective. The potential for blind spots is reduced because they are open to feedback and connected.

The importance of such individuals to help organisations thrive in the 21st century is neatly summarised by Graham Leicester and Maureen O'Hara:

> *Complex problems involving other human beings have no simple answers. They call for judgement, experience, empathy, personal investment, even wisdom – the capacities of whole persons.*[86]

The opposite of this wholeness and integrity is incompleteness[87] in the sense of one who has limited capacity to consider perspectives other than his or her own. The behaviours of a person who is not whole will be defensive and, at worst, paranoid. Potential is necessarily reduced because of heightened subjectivity from a protective, defensive outlook. At the time of writing examples in the political sphere are evident across the globe but of greater relevance will be the examples you can conjure yourself. Who are the best leaders you have encountered? And the worst? If there was a spectrum of integrity and wholeness how would you place them along that scale?

New models of leadership

Jim Collins' book *Good to Great*[88] described the concept of a level 5 leader – the type of leader most likely to sustain great results in a company. In contrast to a "genius with a thousand helpers"[89], a defining characteristic of the level 5 leader is the combination of ambition for the company (not for self) and personal humility.

GBL's formulation of great leadership is someone who is able to create leaders from their followers. These leaders acknowledge others' contribution to success and cultivate great leadership in their team thus building in sustainability for the organisation. This exponentially builds and sustains development in every sense as the focus becomes not the leader (defending the top spot, courting status, preserving individual power) but instead what they are working for, the bigger picture. This enlightened perspective means they will constantly create other torchbearers who will travel further than them, sustaining positive impact long after they are gone.

One of the challenges of recognising let alone appointing such leaders is that it is still common to think of a strong leader as someone quite ruthless and whose aggressive, sometimes unhinged behaviour is tolerated and perhaps even admired by some. We do not need to look far in the business or political arena to see the devastating impact of their legacy. Part of cultivating this whole, integrated-person-leadership is changing our model of what constitutes a leader – not condemning ourselves to live and work as commodities but as fully integrated human beings. Jim Collins' book was first published in 2001, and the lessons on humility and leadership are still relevant today.

Wholeness and the organisation

The Discovery Prism© seeks to connect the dots not just between the different lenses of the framework but also between the individual and the organisation. This is not just by extension (e.g. you are part of this organisation therefore you will buy in to what it is about) but through a process of engagement and participation (because you are part of this organisation you influence what it can become). The rationale for the existence of the Discovery Prism© is that for an organisation to become a leading, thriving 21st century organisation, it also needs to become fully integrated. Changing the final word in the quotation on page 185 to read "organisations" rather than "persons" illustrates the logic of this connection:

> *Complex problems[90] involving other human beings have no simple answers. They call for judgement, experience, empathy, personal investment, even wisdom – the capacities of whole [organisations][91].*

How we harness that *judgement, experience* and *empathy* and deploy our personal investment to come to a new knowing which increases the capacity of the organisation is the question the Discovery Prism© seeks to answer on an individual and collective level.

The richness of the gifts yielded by the Prism is dependent on various elements which are categorised as follows:

- Elevating the status of being
- Collaborative practice
- Encouraging dialogue
- Connecting the dots

1. Elevating the status of being

The previous chapters describe how each lens included in the Discovery Prism© has earned its place in the framework. On reviewing the framework, one global HR professional covered up the top circle and remarked that the typical focus for most companies is what is left as seen below: vision, strategy and mission/stakeholders.

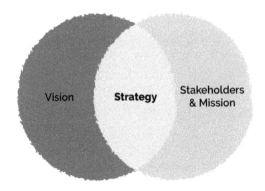

Figure 22 **The bit that most companies consider**

"The other lenses," she continued, "bigger purpose, values, legacy and promises, often get missed and yet are so important." When asked what the result would be for her when they were fully integrated, she replied: "Trust. You would lose the *what ifs* in your head and just give your all."

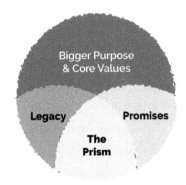

Figure 23 **The bit that's normally missed**

The activity of creating a present organisation, making the being and doing coherent, is work that helps to get rid of the "What ifs" (what if they're not telling us the truth about where this initiative will take us, what if they're planning to get rid of us once we've instigated all the efficiencies, what if we put all this work in and then they change it all over again...). In his book *Create A World That Works* Alan Seale talks of two orientations of awareness, one on the Vertical (Being) and the other on the Horizontal (Doing) plane, and he represents these on a cross[92].

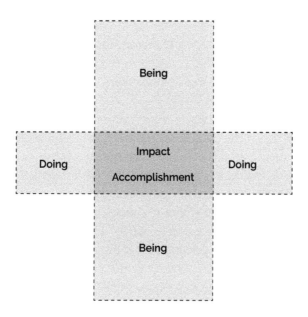

Figure 24 **Alan Seale's Being and Doing Planes**

Although things are changing, Seale explains how traditionally the focus in the West is on doing – achievement, actions and tangible results. He acknowledges that while these are important, growth, systemic transformation and sustainable accomplishment must be congruent with the vertical plane – the being. This does not mean that results and performance are not important. It does mean that if we have tunnel vision on results without developing awareness of our thoughts, beliefs, intentions, attitudes and perspectives, then results are short term, without roots, or not sustainable. Consider the story in the chapter on purpose from the doctors' group[93] – focusing on a bigger purpose leads to better results than the initial rigid focus on the bottom line.

Extraordinary Leadership have created a tool called ACT[94] which stands for Awareness, Connection and Transformation.

Awareness

ACT   **Connection**

Transformation

Figure 25 **ACT from Extraordinary Leadership**

The quality of each stage determines the quality of the subsequent one. The quality of your awareness will determine the quality of your connection, and the quality of your connection will determine the quality of your capacity to transform. Reflecting on this exercise, a leadership development participant realised he'd been trying to transform his team without awareness of their challenges or without connection to them. It just doesn't work this way. It's like expecting to win the lottery without buying a ticket. Thriving in a 21ˢᵗ century world is about sustainability[95] in the human and environmental arenas. Sustain your people, sustain your environment; these create and sustain results. When you have worked through the Discovery Prism© framework you will have gained both awareness and connection. The potential transformation is what you uncover at the core – the Prism itself. GBL defines transformation as a shift in thinking/feeling/ perception, which renders the previously impossible, possible. This cannot be done without alignment of the Being and the Doing, without Awareness and Connection. Alan Seale sums this up as follows:

When there is no personal meaning or connection between the project or goal and the people involved, the project is not likely to be sustainable. Sustainability requires meaning and connection. However, when your action in the horizontal (Doing) plane is informed by intuitive awareness, insight and alignment with the big-picture view of the vertical (Being) plane, and rooted in meaning and personal motivation, you can accomplish incredible things.[96]

In the Discovery Prism©, the being is represented mainly by purpose and values (although there are elements of "being" present in all the lenses). We are consciously bringing them to the fore and together. Inviting input on purpose/values/legacy/promises and vision brings the personal into the ring. How can you put your whole self into an endeavour if your "self" is not represented or visible? When we sense our organisation does not represent us, we distance ourselves psychologically. A common example of this is the practice of mocking the vision/mission/values statements to express dissent for what doesn't represent you. The Prism can also pinpoint what is not working, is incoherent or failing to yield the results it should.

The being is also implicit in how we explore the lenses. How are you when you are participating in the exploration? How do you create the environment which leads to this alignment? It's not just about what you focus on but how you focus. This is where the importance of collaboration and dialogue come in.

2. Collaborative practice

We have included the following quotes from Graham Leicester and Maureen O'Hara because they underline the importance of participation and practice for organisations of tomorrow.

Organisation is a means of getting things done. But it is also a way of living together. The value of an organizational setting that embodies the qualities of persons of tomorrow can only be gained through participation and experience. It cannot be bought. It is like learning a language: the only way to do so is to practice, in the company of others.[97]

Working collaboratively by understanding the layered purposes of the system is a way of leveraging the organisation's capacity to work effectively in the complex 21st century environment.

Collaboration across boundaries is necessary to maintain stability within and among groups. When members can achieve a state where they become attuned to each other and to purposes of the whole, a group can play well above its weight. There is an almost uncanny level of expanded knowledge available to them and they find they can handle complex and ill-defined problems beyond the capacity of any of the individual members.[98]

If the Discovery Prism© is anything, it is a participative activity. Participative at the level of the individual – bringing his or her whole self, his or her presence – to the dialogue; participative at the level of it being holistic in its components (see the being and doing); also participative in the breadth of its invitation to the organisation. The wider the net is cast to encourage that participation, the more far-reaching the power of the Prism. In most organisations these conversations don't take place at all and at best perhaps the senior team provides input. The senior team then find themselves having to put in an inordinate amount of energy to "sell" the vision or the values to the rest. Great investment has been made in branding so now everyone must be told what's important to them. (The fact that a great investment has been made is never a good selling point to the consumer.) Unfortunately, unless those values resonate, this backwards approach is often a waste of money and resources with everyone noticing the cavern between the ideas they're sold and the reality they experience.

A concern of casting the net widely may be the complexity of handling multiple and diverse input. There may be questions about how anything can be synthesised from multiple contributors from multiple perspectives. In well-facilitated groups where people are heard, main themes do funnel. As people understand each other more, distances are breached. We have facilitated in organisations where natural barriers exist along departmental lines. Sales teams are pitched against credit analysts for example. Yet when there is dialogue rather than debate the openness and understanding that follows provides the platform for a completely different relationship. For this collaboration to flourish rather than flounder the practice of dialogue is key.

3. Encouraging dialogue

> *Dialogue does not require people to agree with each other. It encourages people to participate in a pool of shared meaning that leads to aligned action[99]...*

> *In dialogue you're not building anything, you're allowing the whole that exists to become manifest. It's a deep shift in consciousness away from the notion that parts are primary.[100]*

We have few role models in any sphere showing us what dialogue is in practice. Instead the norm is adversarial debate where the most articulate person wins the day. Unless you want to wind up in the same place you started, you need to be able to open up conversations rather than close them down. What is needed is a mindset of curiosity, of what could be discovered, rather than a mindset of imposition and certitude. It means expanding the conversation rather than bringing it to a point. It means inviting a person to expand their thinking so you can better understand, and in this process people end up understanding themselves better.

Instead of getting self-interested views (i.e. from the person/ team who carries the day), you are looking for what expresses the whole. A strategy can look good on paper, but unless it relates to what key stakeholders want or need or has the capacity to deliver the vision, what use is it? Connecting the dots for congruent action is key.

In talking about collaboration and dialogue people often worry that the output is watered-down compromise or consensus. We are used to either democracy or autocracy to deliver a decisive response but neither of these are of themselves necessarily collaborative, holistic or emergent.

Dialogue and collaboration are about keeping us in the "doing the right things right" box (in the chapter on strategy). They are about reducing the influence of personal agendas and egos on key decisions. They are about being in areas that matter to stakeholders, hearing, understanding, listening for the wisdom that emerges. They are about eliciting the wisdom (not the acquiescence) of all participants. The practice of collaboration and dialogue holds the power to cut through complexity even though at the start it may seem you are increasing it by inviting participation. A fellow coach related how a CEO following the 2008 crash was boasting how the downturn had provided the opportunity to get rid of dead wood. "Dead wood?" the coach replied. "Do you hire dead wood, or did you hire live wood and kill it?" Dialogue and collaboration, internal and external to the organisation, are two approaches that assume you have live wood and want to keep it living.

4. Connecting the dots

Seeing things whole "amounts to an inner shift in awareness and consciousness".[101]

The childhood game we've doubtless all played involved joining numbered dots to complete a picture. The potential for the picture to emerge is always there but you need to connect the dots in the right sequence to see the reward of the completed image.

A legitimate question with reference to teams or organisations could be what is the picture you want to emerge, what are you connecting the dots for? For powerful and effective impact connect:

- Your inner voice to action rather than to stagnation
- Mind to body and spirit, and body and spirit to mind
- Intellect and technical expertise to emotional intelligence
- Attention to intention and impact
- Organisational values to behaviours to results
- People development to the needs of the business
- People and teams across functions, cultures and generations
- The head and the heart of the organisation to all of its stakeholders
- Short to longer term vision
- Vision to purpose
- Current self to potential self; current team to potential team; current organisation to potential organisation

Connecting the dots is another vital part of the wholeness and integrity spoken about at the beginning of the chapter. Finding the first dot, number one, is important. Without this connection to the current situation, there is no platform to springboard towards what's possible. If people cannot trust they are at the right departure point then how can they be inspired by where their journey might take them? This awareness provides the safety and security to step out to the potential that waits to be discovered (and relates to the type of safety Joan Planes refers to below which emerges at the Prism, the overlap of all of the lenses).

Connecting dots to create a recognisable image fulfils the subconscious human need for pattern recognition and completion. When clarity is lacking (regarding purpose, our role, the bigger picture) people become frustrated, lack motivation and don't perform at their best. They are equally dissatisfied when they have started something that is interrupted and are unable to bring it to satisfactory closure. We are hard-wired for connection and yet we don't always notice when we are "out of connection".

An example of what happens when the dots are not connected is that departments can become silos of non-cooperation pitching battles against each other for resources, or competitive entities fighting to obtain their own strategic goals at the cost of other departments. Energy and resources are deployed in fighting internally rather than harnessing the collective for superlative results. History shows internecine wars are far bloodier than those fought across external borders. How can any organisation afford this dissipation?

Connecting the dots across teams, departments, geography and stakeholders is the way to become more attuned and effective.

Conclusion

What emerges at the Prism is always a flow of energy. It is an organisational flow. This is both at the level of the individual and the collective. The way participants will think, feel and be together will be different as a result of exploring the lenses. How does this provide tangible results? Think of it as a communal "can-do attitude", a source of knowing from the collective wisdom, a sense of personal investment for the good of the whole of which you now feel a part rather than apart from. This results in the transformation of humans stepping into potential. In other words there is an observable shift in thinking/feeling/perception, which renders the previously impossible possible. This expansion of perception is a creative output, as seeing something differently means you can create something different as a result.

The aim of connecting the dots is for powerful and effective impact. It's about making your energy count in taking organisations forward in ways which you could not imagine without this energetic attunement. We predict these four elements will become threshold activities in the organisations of tomorrow as more and more people recognise the benefits they bring to the organisation and its people. Our contention is that these practices will pay unexpected dividends in sensing the future and enabling people to work to their full potential together.

FLUIDRA PRESIDENT JOAN PLANES

Helen interviewed **Joan Planes, founder and honorary president of Fluidra** which is a global leader in the swimming pool market with headquarters in Barcelona and 5,500 employees in 45 countries.

As you look back over your life what stands out?

I am happy with what I have achieved. I came from humble beginnings. I'm 76 and still working on social and sustainability projects – I could never have imagined all that I have been able to work on and achieve.

What's been most important to you?

I feel as though I have worked honourably within the companies. I was always close to the employees and part of the team. I had very clear goals – it's really important that employees know your vision and purpose, so you have to be close to them.

As founder of the business, I naturally grew with it as did those who started with me. In contrast, many of today's pyramidal structures are top down – the CEO doesn't necessarily have this relationship with his/her employees. I was someone with a clear vision and a great team to help me build it – I wouldn't change any of that.

What does sustainability mean to you?

There was no such thing as environmental sustainability in 1969 when I started – it's a new concept but what I always ensured was human sustainability – many of the people who started with me have stayed until their retirement from the company.

For the last fifteen to twenty years I have worked closely with the Barcelona Chamber of Commerce and became increasingly engaged in giving back to society.

I am especially proud of what we are achieving in Cepex (plastic pipe and fittings manufacturers and part of the Fluidra group). We adhere to lean and zero waste principles. Cepex really looks after people, understanding what tires them and minimising these factors. It's not just that we know that a happier worker is a more productive one – we are genuinely concerned with people's welfare. We've evolved a lot in terms of what it is to look after people and the environment and this is really important to me. I do think in general, companies are becoming more human.

I am a bit "anti-business schools". I feel their graduates haven't lived and breathed a company as I have where you've experienced the first, second and maybe even the third skin of an organisation. I feel that professionals with a particular area of expertise, say marketing or sales, come into a company and build their own micro-climate rather than connecting across the company. I remember my disappointment upon meeting the CEO of a large company in the same market as ours in the US. I asked him how many skimmers they manufactured and he didn't even know they manufactured skimmers let alone how many. I wondered how he could be close to his employees not even knowing what they were working on. CEOs can easily lose sight of their own humanity. They have international profiles and want to wield power and influence at the cost of others. They have to remember they are no different to anyone else. A simple person can be the happiest and the most powerful.

What is gained when there is alignment between vision, purpose, values, stakeholders and mission?

There is a plus. What is the plus? I feel when purpose/vision/values are aligned it's being attuned. Your employees and clients are completely attuned – it's something that is palpable, almost like electric vibrations which the person with you can feel. This gives a sense of security to those that perceive it, you are on the same wave length – it's an energy, it can be felt.

My legacy?

I feel my legacies are those things I have created that are sustainable and will be here in the future when I am not. Fluidra, a successful company, is one, the restored church which serves its community through music and art is another. I am currently developing the concept of corporate music which I hope will unify the company – the music will involve water and is part of our common identity. I am also working with some youngsters in Senegal helping to build a better future for them. Personally, the most important thing at 76 and knowing that my cancer could re-emerge at any time, is to be satisfied with what I have done and to be able to face death with courage and peace.

Helen was very moved to hear Joan Planes' story – how he used the word *sintonia* in Spanish to describe the "plus" – the Prism in terms of our framework. This translates exactly to attunement. Attunement goes beyond alignment, but is the result of alignment, of congruence, coherence, and deep connection. Because attunement is felt beyond our five senses as a vibrational energy it is beyond the three-dimensional. It is the Prism, the overlap of all the lenses. We believe this is possible within organisations small and large.

The Discovery Prism© framework reveals that prioritising what is important brings comprehensive and unexpected dividends.

A TALE FROM THE RIVERBANK

Interview with **Andy Mitchell, CEO of Thames Tideway Tunnel, London.**

> *It might sound cheesy but as a chief exec I need to talk about the importance of being brave, human and our love affair with the river.*

Tideway is the company delivering the Thames Tideway Tunnel, London's new 25 km long "super sewer", which will prevent millions of tonnes of sewage entering the River Thames.

This organisation serves as a best practice example on many accounts. It operates in a complex environment with a broad range of stakeholders to satisfy from the private, public and governmental sector. It displays the kind of 21st century leadership practices that may not normally be associated with the construction and engineering industry.

Andy Mitchell, the chief executive of Tideway, has many years' experience of running large construction projects (like Crossrail in the UK, Europe's biggest infrastructure project). This was the first time, as CEO, he had the luxury of starting with a clean sheet. Above all he wanted to create an organisation where people thrive, in the firm belief that if they do, they excel in their approach to work and deliver stellar performance. He was keen to focus on the "how" as much as the "what", understanding that the emotional platform is what enables people to perform at their absolute best. *"We would not be where we are today had we not been* **how** *we are".*

In the first months Andy spent time asking questions, talking to people, listening to their thoughts and ideas. Above all he pushed the message "We are the masters of our own destiny. We can be what we want to be." In order to capture thoughts and ideas, a creative space (with green astroturf, a white picket fence and scribbling wall) was allocated, accessible to all. People were to imagine what the Thames could be; anything was allowed, the wackier the better. They could write their ideas on two tables in response the question: "If this was the best company in the world what would we do?" His idea was to cut people loose from their bounded thinking and open them up to dream. To put this in context, many had already experienced five years of the consultation process with legal, precise, technical engineering language. He needed to give people the permission to think wider, express feelings and use words that were uncommon in their work vocabulary. This common language would build the base for a new, open, collaborative culture.

After the creative gathering phase a series of workshops was run to define the essence of what the organisation is doing and what it stands for, its mission and purpose. This is not about building a tunnel, this is about creating value for a wide community, but how best to put this into words? Andy fondly recounts the moment that, having spent a lot of session time trying to find the best way of describing their ambition, Danny, an engineer said "what we are about is reconnecting people with the river". In Andy's words: "This is all about the emotional connection – it's about a city's love affair with its river."

Andy is not a fan of vision and mission statements on the wall. He finds that people neither remember nor connect to them. He believes instead that key messages should be communicated by each and every individual in their own way. So that's what he encouraged, by asking people to write down what the vision "we reconnect people with the river" means to them personally. People outside the company report that regardless of whom they talk to in Tideway they speak with passion; it's about a common story, and it's in their own words. What is very tangible is the sense of being connected to the cause.

If values had been chosen these would be empathy, sympathetic, caring – this is the distilled essence from all the stories (and Andy exudes this!). He is running a four billion pound construction project and says himself that "it's built on emotion".

"What comes first is the emotional piece. That's what drives people."

Andy's leadership principles are inclusive; he champions diversity throughout the organisation (and there are plenty of examples that illustrate this). He enables collaboration across all levels, wanting to remove hierarchical boundaries – a command and control culture is not in evidence in this organisation. *"Control? I never had it. I don't want it!"*

A project team of volunteers from all levels in the organisation were responsible for the office move in London to a Thames riverside location that was more representative of all the company stands for. In the early days of planning Andy needed to push back on requests for permission and encouraged the team to take its own decisions. He first viewed the new premises four weeks before the 300 people moved in and was delighted by what he saw.

Andy encourages innovation and thinks people should be allowed to fail. *"If someone isn't making mistakes, they aren't getting out and trying stuff. You have to dare. And to dare not to ask permission is part of this."*

Apart from being proud of the futuristic Thames-side offices, he is keen to report that Tideway has a pilot "flagship" site office that is "everything a construction office has never been!"

Andy keeps himself from becoming too entrenched in his ways by hiring leaders he hasn't worked with before (rather than taking tried and tested resources from previous projects). He wants to see people run past him; this spurs him to increase his pace to keep up. He acknowledges that his job is done when people feel they can do their jobs to the best of their ability. *"If you employ people with passion and give them the space, they will excel."*

Three years after starting as the CEO, after the move to the new office, Andy had the two original tables with all the thoughts and ideas removed from storage. What Tideway had become as an organisation was what was described on the tables. "We fancifully said, this is how we'd like it to be. Without consciously doing it, without a defined plan of action or follow-up, we had become what we are." Their culture had emerged from the "sense" of the hopes that had been written down. As the architect of this, Andy's job is done. People "get it".

Tideway's legacy? This encompasses the lives of the six million people that live next to the river and the six million tourists that come every year. "If we achieve the biggest value for society in what we are doing, people will look back and feel differently."

QUESTIONS FOR REFLECTION

What emerges from the other lenses?

? What is the truth that needs to be spoken?
? What is the shift that needs to be enabled?
? What is disconnected that needs to be connected?

From which other questions follow, for example:

? What is the prize?
? What is the potential for you/your team/organisation right now?
? Who are you and your team/your organisation being asked to be?
? What is the potential asking you and your team/your organisation to do?
? What compromises claiming the prize?
? What is the shadow/negative side of where you are now?
? Who do you leave behind?
? When are your values compromised?
? When do you lose clarity?
? What are your/your team's default, unhelpful behaviours?
? What/whom are you being loyal to that does not serve your purpose?

CHAPTER SUMMARY

Here are the main points of Chapter 8:

> The meaning of the Prism as a metaphor for the collective energy of the people in an organisation which enables transformation

> The importance of integrated leaders who enable an expanded outlook and create leaders of their followers paving the way for integrated organisations

> The four elements of working which hold the key to creating an integrated organisation: the being, collaboration, dialogue and connecting the dots

> Examples which describe attunement resulting from integrated organisations

Conclusion

Conclusion

In the previous chapters we have introduced the Discovery Prism© as a framework to structure thinking about the big questions that when explored dynamically in any organisation have the power to transform. Sustainable transformation honours each individual and all stakeholders, now and for the future.

The central idea, represented by the white light of the Prism, is that when all contribute through focused attention, exploring all the key themes, something bigger emerges that imparts a powerful energy. This energy attracts more potential and becomes the source of further creation. The concept of attunement is this sense of affinity with something wider, which is more than the alignment created by the intersection of all lenses.

The Discovery Prism© is about leadership – the integrated leader – who has a sense of him or herself in all the lenses and enables the creation of an integrated organisation. It is also about the organisation as a collective. Leadership is not only practised through formal roles, in the traditional sense of the leader at the top of the organisation or unit. Leadership in the 21st century is about stepping up and being accountable for the part each one of us is called to play in service of something greater. The best conditions for people to thrive in organisations of any kind are those that recognise individual potential and difference and encourage collaboration and dialogue to get best results.

It takes real courage and vulnerability to talk about the things that matter but which are difficult to talk about and to invite participation – who knows what people will say? One of the benefits of working with the Discovery Prism© is that it provides a simple process and approach, asking questions and creating a common language to talk about what is deep and complex. Perhaps the catalyst is knowing you need to tap into something deeper to get something rare but worthwhile.

In this book we have argued for bringing what is important to human beings into the work arena because that is what gets the best results; that is what is most likely to uncover amazing potential across and for a variety of stakeholders. This is what will give rise to superior organisations rather than merely average ones[102].

It is our hope that as a result of reading this book, you will be inspired to apply some of the principles, and in answering the questions posed at the end of each chapter, come closer to your ideal outcomes. These may be the tangibles or intangibles which arise from stronger connections between people, across teams and across organisations.

No matter your purpose in embarking on a journey of discovery for your team or organisation, our wish is that what you discover will be more valuable than you could ever imagine.

As coaches, we are compelled to finish with a question:

What is the more to be discovered?

Glossary

Alignment
Congruence and coherence across one or more of the lenses.

Attuned/Attunement
Deeply synchronised, intuitively on the same wavelength, in flow.

Being
Being as distinct from Doing. The way we are in any situation. The "how" we are which affects what we do, how we do it, how we relate to others and how they relate to us e.g. the difference between being calm, relaxed and centred (grounded being) or being uptight, anxious and confused. Think of how we would act and react differently according to the state of our being in each case.

Bigger purpose
The deepest motivation which drives action.

Circular lens
One of the three complete circle lenses: bigger purpose and core values, vision, stakeholders and mission.

Congruence/Congruent
A sense of alignment, common meaning and consistency across a series of elements. Personal congruence is about authenticity, where a person's values and beliefs are consistent with the way he or she lives her life.

Core values
Concepts which are important to people and which drive behaviours.

Dialogue

Communication which aims to expand understanding of self and others, characterised by asking open questions and focused listening to avoid assumptions.

The Discovery Prism©

The complete framework, all lenses and the Prism at the centre.

Discovery work

Working with the Discovery Prism© framework using the 4 principles: being, collaboration, dialogue and connecting the dots. These principles are practised throughout the 4 stages:

1. Pre-exploration: What is the intention for the upcoming work?
2. Exploring the Discovery Prism©: Creative reflection on the questions through dialogue and collaboration.
3. Connecting the dots: Distilling responses at the Prism to find the common essence. What paths are clear; what is now possible?
4. Sustaining focus: What needs to happen to keep the conversations and connections fluid and relevant and prevent complacency?

Emergent/Emergence

Describes the phenomenon of something being created by the whole which is greater than the sum of the contributory parts e.g. the capacity of an organisation working collaboratively to produce something beyond the levels of expertise and intelligence of the individuals of that organisation.

Energetically (as in "felt energetically")

The difference between knowing something intellectually and feeling it in your body when it arouses all your senses. Normally this is not something we express in words but is expressed in our reactions and in how we act e.g. the difference in the way we work when uninspired or when inspired.

Exploring the lenses

Working on the lenses to gain clarity and make discoveries (see also discovery work).

Fluid versus fixed

Related to strategy, two ends of the same spectrum. The ideal would be to formulate a strategy that can be fixed enough to show consistent direction and fluid enough to adapt to changing circumstances. This is the typical dilemma of working in a matrix organisation.

Grounded

Someone who is focused, centred and present and able to stay in this state no matter the external circumstances.

Holding the space

We are said to be "holding the space" when we are contributing actively to the emergent process. That is we are standing back from our own thoughts and interventions to allow the wisdom of the system to emerge. This can take the form of asking open questions to clarify meaning for all, allowing silence for deeper awareness to emerge, or providing a framework which allows exploration. It is characterised by non-judgement, respect and presence. One or more people can hold the space in this way.

Human sustainability

A culture of recognising and considering the dignity of human beings at the centre of organisational life.

Leader

An individual who is accountable for the delivery of objectives and who enables others to exercise leadership. Most often recognised as the person with title e.g. CEO, MD, Manager. Is also the person without a title or recognised authority who takes responsibility for their impact in advancing the organisation.

Legacy
What is consciously created for future generations.

Lenses
The circular and overlap lenses consisting of bigger purpose and core values; vision; mission and stakeholders; legacy; promises; strategy and the Prism.

Mission
Focusing on today – what your business does to deliver your vision. Mission questions are: what do we do, who do we serve and how? An example of LinkedIn's mission is: To connect the world's professionals to make them more productive and successful.

Other-focused
The capacity to focus on others' needs, emotions, part in the system, as well as self so to connect with, motivate and inspire others.

Overlap lens
The three lenses which emerge from overlaps with the three circular lenses: legacy, promises and strategy.

The Prism
The centre of the framework where all the lenses overlap.

Promises
The alignment between the behaviours arising from core values internally and externally to the organisation.

Stakeholders
The net of individuals and entities impacted by the organisation, both internal and external.

Strategy
A method or plan to marshall resources for their most efficient and effective use to deliver the organisational vision for stakeholders.

Systemic sustainabilty
A culture of recognising and considering the wider impact of the organisation on surrounding communities and the environment.

Systemic team coaching
A process of coaching the whole team, individually and together to deliver the team's purpose, serving all stakeholders who form the wider system of which the team is a part.

Threshold activity
Just as threshold competencies are the basic knowledge, skills and traits for performing a job today, the four principles: being, collaboration, dialogue, connecting the dots will become those basic areas of activity for companies to thrive in the future.

Virtual team
A team that, for the most part, is linked through communication (rather than face to face) by different modes such as email, voicemail, phone, video-conferencing or internet-based forums. This definition means that even "local" teams are virtual! Nearly everyone today works virtually for part if not most of the time.

Vision
A compelling definition of where the organisation is heading tomorrow. An example of LinkedIn's vision: To create economic opportunity for every member of the global workforce.

Whole-system space
The destination of working with the Discovery Prism© framework. A place where participants are aware of the whole-system as a result of the exploration of all the lenses. Here, all the colours are brought together in the prism enabling a new awareness to emerge.

Endnotes

1. Peter M. Senge, Bryan Smith, Joe Laur, Nina Kruschwitz & Sara Schley (2010), *The Necessary Revolution: How Individuals and Organizations are Working Together to Create a Sustainable World*, London/Boston: Nicholas Brealey Publishing, p.10.
2. We refer to soul as essence, spirit, source – the person/team/organisation at their/its deepest level.
3. From the McKinsey report on 21st century leadership. https://www.mckinsey.com/featured-insights/leadership/leading-in-the-21st-century
4. Such as the Global Finance Leader Study: Finance Leaders Share the Top Risks that Matter Most, in *Forbes*, 25 July 2018 https://bit.ly/2NGYMqf
5. In our research we found Mission and Purpose are often interchangeable where the answer to "What are you here to do?" can be synonymous with "Why are you here?" In the Discovery Prism© Mission answers the question of "What do you do to deliver your Purpose?" Whilst acknowledging there are many overlaps between the terminologies, we feel that asking questions from a defined perspective can provide subtly differing and helpful reflections.
6. See footnote 3.
7. Our values dictate how we behave. For more clarification see the section on working with CTT© later in the chapter.
8. For glossary of terms re the framework, please see page 212.
9. Founder and Director Alan Seale at www.transformationalpresence.org.
10. https://www.zappos.com/about/purpose Zappos.com is an online shoe and clothing retailer based in Las Vegas, Nevada.
11. Sir Laurens van der Post in the documentary Hasten Slowly (1997).
12. S. Sinek (2009), *Start With Why: How Great Leaders Inspire Everyone to Take Action*, New York: Penguin Random House.
13. 11th Private Equity Symposium, 24–25 May 2018, https://www.london.edu/faculty-and-research/lbsr/why-it-pays-to-be-socially-responsible-in-business
14. https://www.globaljustice.org.uk/blog/2016/sep/12/corporations-running-world-used-be-science-fiction-now-its-reality
15. From Larry Fink's published letter to CEOs, https://www.blackrock.com/corporate/investor-relations/larry-fink-ceo-letter
16. Source: https://www.soundstrue.com/store/about-us/core-values
17. https://www.london.edu/faculty-and-research/lbsr/why-it-pays-to-be-socially-responsible-in-business

18. Harvard Business Review Analytic Services in collaboration with the EY Beacon Institute, the Business Case for Purpose, https://www.ey.com/Publication/vwLUAssets/ey-the-business-case-for-purpose/$FILE/ey-the-business-case-for-purpose.pdf

19. The State of the debate on purpose in business © 2016 EYGM Limited available at https://www.ey.com/Publication/vwLUAssets/ey-the-state-of-the-debate-on-purpose-in-business/%24FILE/ey-the-state-of-the-debate-on-purpose-in-business.pdf

20. ibid, p.1.

21. From https://www.b.co.uk/what-is-engagement/ (Best Companies)

22. Tom Peters and Robert H. Waterman, 2004, *In Search of Excellence: Lessons from America's Best Run Companies*, London: Profile Books, p. 291. First published by Harper & Row, 1982.

23. Rosabeth Moss Kanter, Chair of the Harvard University Advanced Leadership Initiative, in her article: Adding Values to Valuations: Indra Nooyi and Others as Institution-Builders, *Harvard Business Review*, May 3, 2010, https://hbr.org/2010/05/adding-values-to-valuations-in.html

24. https://www.valuescentre.com/about/barrett-values-centre

25. For an example of the Business Needs Scorecard©, please see page 158 (Strategy Chapter 6).

26. Ronald Cohen, 2007, *The Second Bounce of the Ball: Turning Risk into Opportunity*, UK: Weidenfeld & Nicholson, Chapter 1 (ebook).

27. John F. Kotter (1996) *Leading Change*, Harvard Business Review Press, p.67, p.85, p.101.

28. Peter Drucker, 1988, The Coming of the New Organisation, *Harvard Business Review*, January 1988, https://hbr.org/1988/01/the-coming-of-the-new-organization

29. Deepak Chopra, 2011, *The Soul of Leadership: Unlocking Your Potential for Greatness*, London: Rider ebook, an imprint of Ebury Publishing (Random House Group), Location 271. Originally published by Harmony Books, New York, 2010.

30. Daniel Goleman and Richard E. Boyatzis, 2002, *The New Leaders: Transforming the Art of Leadership*, Time Warner paperback.

31. Tom Rath and Barry Conchie. 2007, StrengthsFinder 2.0. *Strengths based Leadership, Great Leaders, Teams and Why People Follow*, New York: Gallup Press, p.105.

32. Lucy Kellaway in the *Financial Times*, 5 July 2015, available at https://www.ft.com/content/f00b0b08-1f4f-11e5-aa5a-398b2169cf79

33. https://www.wsj.com/articles/twitter-ceo-dick-costolo-struggles-to-define-vision-1415323289

34. Nick Baines, 2013, "Voting for a change", in his blog, Musings of a restless bishop, https://nickbaines.wordpress.com/, March 2, 2013.

35. See www.wellboring.org and www.xleadership.com. Summit Schools now have their own website at www.maraguasummit.com

36. Peter Hawkins, 2011, *Leadership Team Coaching: Developing collective transformational leadership*, London: Kogan Page, Location 438, Part One High-performing Teams, Ch. 1 Why the world needs more high-performing leadership teams.

37. https://mars.nasa.gov/programmissions/missions/future/mars2020/

38. https://www.tablegroup.com/imo/media/doc/AdvantageThe_Last_Competitive_Advantage(4).pdf

39. Frederic Laloux, 2015, "The Future of Management Is Teal", in *Strategy and Business*, Reprint No. 0344, https://www.strategy-business.com/article/00344?gko=10921

40. Morning Star's mission https://bit.ly/2nPi4iF

41. https://www.weareneo.com/what-we-do/

42. Frederic Laloux, 2015, "The Future of Management Is Teal", in *Strategy and Business*, Reprint No. 0344, https://www.strategy-business.com/article/00344?gko=10921

43. https://www.mckinsey.com/featured-insights/leadership/leading-in-the-21st-century

44. Also called the stakeholder influence interest matrix and the power/interest grid.

45. Gartner Research Note Summary, March 2018. How we will work in 2027 (online source no longer available).

46. https://www2.deloitte.com/insights/us/en/focus/executive-transitions/managing-stakeholder-relationships.html

47. Provider: The Academy of Executive Coaching. https://www.aoec.com/training/team-coach-training/team-connect-360/

48. Barry Oshry, 2007, *Seeing Systems: Unlocking the Mysteries of Organizational Life*, 2nd Edition, San Francisco: Berrett-Koehler Publishers, Inc.

49. https://www.canopyadvisory.com/internal-brand-is-your-company-walking-the-talk/

50. CIPD Factsheet https://bit.ly/2MHmYIX

51. Fig 14: Ocean Tomo Intangible Asset Market Value Study, 2017, at http://www.oceantomo.com/intangible-asset-market-value-study/

52. Source: 2018 Edelman Trust Barometer. What consequences are you experiencing as a direct result of the media not doing a good job fulfilling its responsibilities? https://bit.ly/2yADrJq

53. https://alta.bcorporation.uk/about-b-corps

54. https://hbr.org/2016/06/why-companies-are-becoming-b-corporations

55. Article about Glassdoor by Lydia Dishman, 17 July 2015, https://bit.ly/2vScPDp

56. https://worldwork.global/product/international-team-trust-indicator-questionnaire/

57. Frederic Laloux, 2014, *Reinventing Organizations: A Guide to Creating Organizations Inspired by the Next Stage of Human Consciousness*, Brussels: Nelson Parker (ebook).

58. ibid, location 455.

59. A series of short videos by Frederic Laloux that demonstrate the practices of teal organisations: https://thejourney. reinventingorganizations.com/

60. Leandro Herrero, 2011, *Homo Imitans: The Art of Social Infection: Viral Change™ in Action*, Bucks: The Chalfont Project t/a Meeting Minds Publishing.

61. ibid, p.13.

62. In "The Office of Strategy Management" by Robert S. Kaplan and David P. Norton, from the October 2005 issue of the *Harvard Business Review*.

63. See Glossary for definition of virtual team on page 216.

64. https://www.pwc.com/gx/en/ceo-survey/2015/assets/pwc-18th-annual-global-ceo-survey-jan-2015.pdf

65. Frederic Laloux, 2014, *Reinventing Organisations: A Guide to Creating Organizations Inspired by the Next Stage of Human Consciousness*, Brussels: Nelson Parker (ebook), location 4259.

66. In the Production Unit activity, participants are divided into teams of planners and implementers and given a task to perform, under pressure, within a strict time limit. The teams are divided into groups from the outset, but the instructions do not forbid them in any way to join forces in their preparation nor in the execution of their "production run".

67. James Quinn, 1993, "Managing Strategic Change", in Christopher Mabey and Bill Mayon-White, *Managing Change*, 2nd Edition, London: The OU/Paul Chapman Publishing, p.66.

68. James Quinn, 1978, "Strategic change: 'Logical incrementalism'", *Sloan Management Review* 20, 7–19.

69. Cisco, 2011, "The Collaboration Imperative, Executive Strategies for Unlocking your Organization's True Potential", San Jose, California: Cisco Systems, Inc., p. 92.

70. This work is licensed under a Creative Commons Attribution Share-Alike 3.0 License. https://leadingedgeforum.com/advisory-service/wardley-maps/

71. An example of Wardley Mapping about can be found here: https://www.youtube.com/watch?v=M0SCTKmfmtI

72. Ken Wilber, 2007, *The Integral Vision: A Very Short Introduction to the Revolutionary Integral Approach to Life, God, the Universe, and Everything*, Boston/London: Shambhala Publications Inc.

73. Richard Barrett, 2014, Annex 14 "Using the BNS to develop a balanced set of strategy indicators" in *The Values Driven Organisation*, Abingdon: Routledge, p.223.

74. Sunday Times Best companies to work for https://www.b.co.uk/the-lists/

75. Richard Barrett, 2014, "The impact of values on performance" in *The Values Driven Organisation*, Abingdon: Routledge, p.30.

76. Barrett Values Centre, 2015, Financial Services Industry Report, Desired cultural values of Financial Service Industry 2007–2014. Example of Balanced Needs Scorecard© (BNS) is copyright BVC from information that can be accessed by BVC accredited trainers.

77. https://www.strategy-business.com/article/00344?gko=10921

78. Manifestation Wheel from Alan Seale: http://transformationalpresence.org/the-manifestation-wheel/ and also Alan Seale, 2008, *The Manifestation Wheel*, San Francisco: Red Wheel/Weiser, LLC.

79. http://www.sixcrows.org/library/TheMeaningandUseOfThe MedicineWheelByRoyDudgeon.pdf

80. Tom Rath, 2013, *Strengths Based Leadership. Great Leaders, Teams, and Why People Follow*, Washington DC: Gallup Press, p.5.

81. Source: *Economist*, August 25, 2018.

82. Nike nearly dropped Colin Kaepernick before embracing him. https://www.nytimes.com/2018/09/26/sports/nike-colin-kaepernick.html

83. Strava is software used to track cycling, running and swimming activity via GPS.

84. F. Laloux, 2014, *Reinventing Organisations: A Guide to Creating Organizations Inspired by the Next Stage of Human Consciousness*, Brussels: Nelson Parker (ebook), location 4770.

85. arren Bennis, 1989, *On Becoming a Leader*, New York: Addison-Wesley, Introduction.

86. M. O'Hara & G. Leicester, 2012, *Dancing at the Edge: Competence, Culture and Organization in the 21st Century*, Axminster: Triarchy Press, p.6. For further info: http://www.iffpraxis.com/

87. We do not mean here the clinical disorder known as Incompleteness.

88. J. Collins, 2001, *Good to Great*. London: Random House Business Books.

89. ibid, p. 45.

90. A reminder of why the 21st century organisation's problems are particularly complex. See page 30.

91. Our insertion of "organisations" in place of "person".

92. A. Seale, 2011, *Create A World That Works*, San Francisco: Red Wheel/Weiser, LLC, p.25. Diagram reproduced by kind permission of Alan Seale.

93. See page 49.

94. ACT created by Extraordinary Leadership, www.xleadership.com

95. There are two main areas of sustainability; see page 29 in the Introduction.

96. A. Seale, 2011, *Create A World That Works*, San Francisco: Red Wheel/Weiser, LLC, p.26.

97.   M. O'Hara & G. Leicester, 2012, *Dancing at the Edge: Competence, culture and organization in the 21ˢᵗ century*, Axminster: Triarchy Press, p.122, p.6. For further info: http://www.iffpraxis.com

98.   M. O'Hara & G. Leicester, 2012, *Dancing at the Edge: Competence, culture and organization in the 21ˢᵗ century*, Axminster: Triarchy Press, p.90, p.6. For further info: http://www.iffpraxis.com/

99.   J. Jaworski, 1996, *Synchronicity: The Inner Path of Leadership*, San Francisco: Berrett-Koehler Publishers, p.111.

100. J. Jaworski, 1996, *Synchronicity: The Inner Path of Leadership*, San Francisco: Berrett-Koehler Publishers, p.116.

101. J. Jaworski, 1996, *Synchronicity: The Inner Path of Leadership*, San Francisco: Berrett-Koehler Publishers, p.117.

102. "Being versus Doing" – page 25.